What People Are Saying about Jane Evans
and *Raising Children without Going Insane*

Being great friends, and having children of similar ages, I have watched Jane's parenting journey over the years, and her book honestly and humorously reflects this journey. While clearly revealing the passion she has for her own journey as a mother, she gives great insight and easy-to-apply wisdom to all of us who are also on this wonderful parenting adventure. She's not afraid to tackle hard-to-handle issues and yet will leave you empowered and encouraged, knowing you have everything within you to be the best parent for the children God gave you. Parents, you'll love this book and find it impossible to put down! —Darlene Zschech
Author of *Shout to the Lord*
Hillsong Worship Pastor

You hold in your hands a wonderful blend of wit and wisdom. Jane Evans proves that the mysteries, challenges, and delights of motherhood are just as true in the Land Down Under as anywhere else in the world. Her honesty about her own family's pilgrimage brings to life biblical parenting principles in a fascinating read that will greatly encourage and inspire those who are "in the trenches" with the little ones, and not-so-little ones, God has called them to lead. For dads, this book is a great window into the heart and soul of motherhood. —Dr. Wess Stafford,
President/CEO, Compassion International,
Author of *Too Small to Ignore, Why Children Are the Next Big Thing*

As the parents of five children, my wife and I are always interested in any books that will help our family succeed. Jane Evans' new book on child rearing is one of the best. This book is full of practical advice, personal stories, and scriptural truths that will release the "super parent" in you! —Pastor Jentezen Franklin
Senior Pastor, Free Chapel
Author of *Right People, Right Place, Right Plan*

P9-AOV-208

Jane Evans is one of those wonderful people you meet in life, who is refreshing and unpredictable. Sharing in her experiences as a leader, wife, friend, and ultimately as a devoted parent, you will find this book insightful, helpful, and amusing. Jane is a young woman who is not only negotiating her own family successfully, but is in a position of leadership in our nation where she can observe the lives and experience of many and therefore draw wisdom to help others.

—Bobbie Houston
Hillsong Church

Every product that you can buy, from flat-screen televisions to automobiles, comes with a manual that gives the manufacturer's instructions on how to operate, maintain, and repair the product. However, the only new product that does not come with a manufacturer's manual is a baby. It seems as if the Creator demands that we as human parents pursue the knowledge necessary to effectively develop our children.

In this work, *Raising Children without Going Insane,* Jane Evans is a tremendous contribution to this need for a resource parents can benefit from.

Jane Evans is a seasoned mother and established leader. With honesty and candor, she shares her times of triumph and times when she fell short. She is a shining example that you can fulfill God's purposes for your life while successfully raising a family. *Raising Children without Going Insane* is inspiration for all parents who strive to raise children who fulfill their God-given calling. God knew that you would be the best parent for your children, and Jane Evans reminds you that when you feel discouraged and unable to fulfill your role as a mother, He is more than sufficient to help you. This is an enjoyable and inspiring book for all parents. I challenge you to peel the practical wisdom from each page and apply the time-tested principles that guarantee the product of children as righteous seed to their generation. —Myles Munroe
Best-selling author

RAISING CHILDREN

without going insane

RAISING CHILDREN
without going insane

WHITAKER
HOUSE

RAISING CHILDREN WITHOUT GOING INSANE

www.janeevans.org
For speaking engagements and feedback, please e-mail
jane.evans@paradise.asn.au

ISBN: 978-0-88368-724-6
Printed in the United States of America
© 2005 Australia, 2007 by Jane Evans

1030 Hunt Valley Circle
New Kensington, PA 15068
www.whitakerhouse.com

Library of Congress Cataloging-in-Publication Data

Evans, Jane, 1963–
Raising children without going insane / Jane Evans.
p.   cm.
Summary: "A humorous look at motherhood and practical godly advice from the mother of three boys"—Provided by publisher.
ISBN 978-0-88368-724-6 (trade pbk. : alk. paper) 1. Motherhood—Religious aspects—Christianity. I. Title.
BV4529.18.E94 2007
248.8'431—dc22   2007024007

1 2 3 4 5 6 7 8 9 **ЦJ** 12 11 10 09 08 07

Reflections on Motherhood

I lay on my bed and stared in anger and fear at the ceiling above me, my mind in turmoil. I let my emotions take control. Sobs racked my body. I was exhausted, weary to the bone, and under too much pressure for this to happen. I couldn't go on! No, I *didn't want to* go on! This was not the way it was meant to work out! I sobbed again and wished I could turn back time, my mind numb with thoughts of what the future may hold. I wallowed in self-pity. The only thoughts in my head were of survival! I felt as though I was on a twisting rollercoaster ride to nowhere, totally out of control. You know that feeling you get when traveling at breakneck speed in one direction, and all of a sudden, you are whisked around a sharp bend and your body is taken in another direction? It takes a while for the rest of you to catch up! That's exactly how I was feeling.

You see, I had just found out that I was pregnant. Yes, I was forty years old with two teenage boys. And no, it was not exactly a planned pregnancy (not by us, anyway!). I felt sick in the pit of my stomach and let another sob escape unchecked. I had so many plans, so many things I wanted to do, and none of them included another baby! Then, without warning, I felt a wave of peace and that familiar still, small voice whispered, "Will you do it all again…just for Me?"

I melted. How could I resist? How could I have been so selfish to think this was about me? I dissolved again in another flood of tears, but this time they were tears of surrender, tears that came from someone who knew what she had just been asked to do. This was far bigger than I, far bigger than what I wanted to do with my life. It was about someone else's life; the precious life created in God's heart, nurtured in my womb, and entrusted to my care.

> ## God didn't just see a baby, He saw the man he would become.

Before the foundations of the earth were laid, God knew every detail of this special life he was entrusting to me. He didn't just see a baby. He saw the man he would become. He knew we would call him Benjamin, meaning "son of my right hand." I have the sense that, just as Moses blessed the tribe of Benjamin, God whispered His promise over this special life:

> *The beloved of the Lord shall dwell in safety by Him, who shelters him all the day long; and he shall dwell between His shoulders.* (Deuteronomy 33:12)

When it came time for this life to be formed, God scanned the earth with His eyes, asking,

Whom can I trust to shape and mold someone so precious? Who will take this gift I give them, protecting and nurturing him for Me until it is time to release him into the destiny I have planned for him?

His eyes were searching, then they stopped and rested on a weak and selfish woman; a woman who longed to be all she was created to be, but who many times fell short; a woman far from perfect, but who, sensing her complete inadequacy for the task, would call out to God, allowing Him to exchange her weakness for His strength. I surrendered to the task God was calling me to and clung to Him for strength. The only thing that keeps the roller coaster from going into orbit and destroying its occupants is the fact that its wheels are fixed firmly to the tracks. To be honest, I felt like the only thing keeping me from spinning into orbit was the fact that my "wheels" were firmly connected to Jesus.

I hear you saying that I should never have allowed myself to feel so upset. "How could you have even thought, *I don't want to be pregnant?*" you might ask. "Just imagine the damage you could have done to your baby even thinking that!" Of course, in my situation, you would have been full of joy and thanksgiving. Your heart would have leapt with gratitude for the opportunity to be pregnant again. So what if there was a thirteen-year gap between your last child and this one? What a wonderful present for your teenagers, right? I heard it all in that first week—well-meaning people saying all those well-meaning things. Many of them were right in their own way, but it didn't change the fact that I was upset and needed time to work through my emotions without being told it was wrong to feel them.

> How could I have even thought, *I don't want to be pregnant?*

Unfortunately, I'm not one of those people who breeze through pregnancy, glowing and full of energy. From almost the moment of conception, I feel like I have a terminal illness!

When I'm not pregnant, I have very bad varicose veins; when I'm pregnant, they are horrendous. It is agony to stand for even five minutes, and at the end of the day, my legs are so sore and swollen that I have lie with them up the wall for at least half an hour. And the night cramps are excruciating! Anyway, I'm not trying to make you feel sorry for me, but I didn't know how I was going to get through the following nine months, let alone the years of parenting I had ahead of me! I'd been here twice before. I knew exactly the kind of commitment, resolve, strength, and determination I would need. As far as I was concerned, I didn't know where I was going to find it! Nevertheless, God still thought I had it in me, so who was I to argue?

> Motherhood is a privilege, challenge, heartache, and joy—all at once.

I continued to lie on my bed and, as the peace of God settled around me, I reflected on my fifteen years of motherhood. My journey as a mother has been far from perfect, but always rich and profound. God has provided so many opportunities for growth and transformation in my life by trusting me with the task of raising my sons. As my thoughts meandered through so many lessons and experiences, I was reminded that motherhood is a privilege, challenge, heartache, and joy—all at once. Often it seems like plain hard work, but every moment is worth it. Being a mother requires that you share your life in exchange for the insight gained from loving deeply and unselfishly.

It is a risk to commit to paper some of my insights and reflections on motherhood. In writing about motherhood, I am putting both myself and my children under scrutiny. Still, it is a risk I feel compelled to take. I am definitely not the perfect mother. I don't have perfect kids—trust me, there are plenty of people who would agree with me! So if you are looking for formulas for raising children who behave flawlessly and don't belch at the dinner table, or if you are looking for ten ways to keep from losing your temper at your kids, then this is probably not the book for you. Rather, if you want to hear about another completely human mother's journey, lessons I've learned along the way, things I've done wrong, and things that have worked, then read on.

I do not want to write this book when I am eighty, when my insights seem irrelevant to the generation I am writing for. I look around now and see so many mothers who, like me, through trial and error, are trying their best to do the hardest job on earth. Many of them feel just as I did when discovering that I was to be a mother for the third time—that life has them hurtling along on a roller coaster. It's okay—you're not alone! I hope these reflections will inspire you to parent with confidence, being assured that you have a mandate from God and that you are equipped with everything you need to succeed.

You can have a great journey as a mother and enjoy your kids (most of the time, anyway!). You can do what God placed you on this planet to do without compromising your children's emotional or spiritual health; you can even do all this and still retain your sanity! Besides, God is counting on you to love your kids, because there will be plenty of times when no one else will!

Contents

Help! He's a Warrior!

Parenting the Strong-Willed Child

Help! He's a Warrior!

Parenting the Strong-Willed Child

"In war there is no substitute for victory."
— Douglas MacArthur

The door slammed, and the rhythmic thud of a basketball being bounced on the tiled floor told me Mark, my eldest son, was home. Seconds later, the stereo in his room exploded into sound and the silence was completely shattered.

My oldest son, Mark Samuel, was fifteen when I found out that I was pregnant for the third time. *Mark* means "a mighty warrior" or "a large hammer." (Note to self: always check what a name means before you bestow it upon a child...and yourself!) He has certainly lived up to his name. He is feisty, confident, opinionated, and fearless as a lion. He was born to conquer, but first he had to be conquered!

He started fighting from the moment he was born. The doctor said Mark owed his life to the fact that he was fighter.

Everything went wrong as far as births go. I had an epidural that didn't work properly. The anesthetic traveled upward, rendering me incapable of much movement, but it did nothing to relieve the pain below. We didn't know at the time, but the umbilical cord was wrapped firmly around Mark's neck so that every time I pushed, the tension on the cord began to choke the life out of his little body. I had been pushing for ages but had made very little progress.

His pulse rate dropped and stayed well below 100 for over an hour. The doctor wasn't present and the midwife (bless her!) said to me, "You are not trying hard enough, Mrs. Evans!" I was beginning to get distressed, and the baby was in obvious distress. When the doctor arrived, he threw the midwife out of the room (which was exactly what I would have done if I could!). He called for forceps and for the team to prepare the operating room for an emergency Caesarian. I looked around the room; there was a resuscitation team for me and a resuscitation team for my baby. (I could tell because I was a nurse… sometimes being a nurse doesn't help!)

My husband, Ashley, was wonderful. He has always been great in a crisis and immediately took charge. He encouraged me to give just one more push, and push I did. Mark shot out of me (creating his own opening on the way out!), and the doctor barely had time to catch him. Despite being a dark shade of purple when he was born, he took one massive gulp of air and screamed at the top of his lungs. He had fought to live and has never stopped fighting since.

He was, and still is, one of the strongest-willed children I have ever met. From day one, he screamed for his milk as soon as he felt the pangs of hunger, and the scream didn't stop until the need was met. If I took too long to change his diaper, he would scream in protest. If he was lifted out of a bath he was enjoying—you guessed it—he would scream at the top of his lungs. I had to be very strong with him right from the very beginning. I knew I was in for an interesting ride when, at nine months old, he stamped his foot at me and shouted "No!" to a command I had given him. He crawled early, spoke early, and walked at nine-and-a-half months.

Strong-Willed Children Test You to See How Strong You Are

I have learned, though, that strong-willed children, far from wanting you to give in to them, are actually testing you to see how strong you are. They are longing to know that there is someone out there who is bigger and stronger than they are. When they find someone who will stand up to them and give them strict boundaries, it actually makes them feel safe. A strong-willed child without strong boundaries will always be insecure (in fact, any child without clear boundaries will struggle to feel secure).

> A strong-willed child without strong boundaries will always be insecure.

After each battle, which normally left us both in tears, I would pick him up and put him on my knee and just rock him, telling him that I loved him. These times became known as our "rocking cuddles." Many times when he was hurt or sick, the wounded warrior would come to me, his little face trying to be brave, and ask me for a "rocking cuddle." Here he felt he could cry, his face buried in my shoulder, preventing the world from seeing his fear or his pain. You see, he does feel things deeply; he just doesn't always have the right way of expressing it.

I remember one of his first encounters with my dad. Mark was three at the time. My mother and father lived in the country, so they only saw the boys a few times a year. Each time they had to become reacquainted all over again. Dad was tired, and he and Mom had come to Adelaide for a break. We went away together to the beach for a few days' respite while Ashley was away. Dad, who was exhausted, paid little attention to Mark. Mark missed his daddy and was desperate for some male attention, but he found Grandpa distant and distracted. After several attempts to "play" with Grandpa, who was reading a newspaper, Mark went up to him and kicked him in the shins as hard as he could. Now Grandpa is a warrior too, and an interesting few minutes ensued as I tried to keep these two warriors apart! The funny thing is that they have been best friends ever since. Grandpa took Mark on adventures the next day. They climbed hills together, and at one point a freak wave nearly washed them off some rocks. Grandpa had to hold Mark above his head to stop him from getting wet. Both their faces glowed when they returned and told me the story. Grandpa had found a kindred spirit and Mark had found a hero!

I have cried more than my fair share of tears over this boy. In fact, there was a time when the tears flowed nearly every day. One day, when he was about eighteen months old, I was on my hands and knees cleaning the bathroom when Mark came up to me and called my name. He had Ashley's baseball bat in his hands and swung it at me just as I looked up. The bat connected with the side of my head and I sprawled backward into the shower, stars circling my head as I stared at him in shock. He dropped the bat and burst into tears at what he had done. I was desperate. Sometimes I would look into his eyes and they seemed to be crazed. At times I would wonder if there was some other force at work in him. At other times a fear that he was sick and battling some insidious disease gnawed at my mind.

Allergies and Adrenaline Rushes

It wasn't long before I made the discovery. Shortly after the baseball bat incident, I gave him a drink of chocolate milk and put him in his bed for a nap. Within a few minutes I could hear strange sounds coming from the baby monitor. I hurried into his room to find his face swollen in a hive-like rash. The rash quickly spread to his thighs and upper arms. His breaths came in rasping gasps. My nursing experience told me he was experiencing an allergic reaction to something, so I raced him to the hospital for treatment. It wasn't until some days later that I noticed whenever I gave him milk or milk-based products his behavior changed radically. Then a rash would appear, followed by hives and swelling. Fortunately, I had a knowledgeable general practitioner, and we soon learned that he had numerous food allergies, including an allergy to one of the eight proteins found in cow's milk. The doctor warned us that when we took him off milk-based products

> There is a very fine line between a leader and a rebel. Most rebels are leaders whom someone has given up on.

he may have a reaction similar to what a drug addict experiences coming off drugs. He was right! The milk had been like a drug giving him an adrenaline rush, and his body would experience a "down" feeling when it wore off. This produced

21

in him a subconscious desire for whatever gave him the "up" feeling. No wonder he was addicted to cheese!

We took him off all milk products and, just as the doctor had predicted, it was a very trying two weeks for all of us. He banged his head on the walls; we had to hold him screaming and writhing in our arms until he eventually fell asleep, exhausted. During this two-week period he was irritable and even more erratic than usual, but eventually he calmed down and we began to see a completely different child emerge, one who gradually began to respond.

However, despite the change, Mark was still by no means an easy child. Just before his fourth birthday, I remember calling out to God and declaring that this discipline "thing" wasn't working. There seemed to be absolutely no response to what I was doing...he just seemed to fight harder. Exhausted, I got to the point where I was tempted to give up. Maybe other people were right when they said some children just don't respond to anything. "It doesn't work!" I whined to God. His only answer was to direct me back to Proverbs again, so I underlined every verse that spoke about children. God seemed to be saying, "Don't you trust My Word?" I made a decision that day to continue to trust God and His Word.

I Led My Little Warrior in the Sinner's Prayer

A few weeks later, almost to the day of his fourth birthday, he began to change. Something seemed to be getting through. One day, as I stood in the kitchen doing the dishes, he came up behind me and began to ask me questions about heaven. As clear as anything, that still, small voice said, "Stop what you are doing and talk to him." I sensed this was a God moment, so I took Mark into his room and began to answer his questions about how you get to heaven. I told him that in order to get to heaven you needed to accept Jesus into your life and to believe that He was the Son of God and that He died to forgive you of all the wrong things you had done. I told him that you simply pray a prayer and ask God to take over your life and live inside you. His little eyes widened and he said to me, "Mom, I better do that right now!" (He was always in a hurry!) We knelt together that day, tears streaming down my face, as I led my warrior in the sinner's prayer. He got up and promptly changed the subject, and that was that. From that day on, I noticed a change in his behavior. He became softer, and any time someone talked about Jesus, Mark would say, "He's in my heart!"

> When that still, small voice instructs you to stop and talk to your child, realize it might be a God moment.

Can I encourage you with the words of a man who, against all odds, defeated the enemy marching toward his country: "Never, never, never give up!" It worked for Winston Churchill…and it can work for you! There is an enemy who is intent on destroying your child, an enemy who is after your child's soul, and who is intent on pulling your child off the course that God has set for your child. Part of that strategy is to make you feel discouraged and lose sight of the mandate that God has given you, to make you feel like a failure as a parent and tempt you to give up. That enemy, Satan, whispers the lie I hear from so many mothers' mouths: "They are sixteen now. You can't really tell them anything. I guess they will just have to learn the hard way." I tell my sons that, until they walk down the aisle with the woman God brings into their lives, it is my responsibility before God to watch over their souls. Too many parents relinquish that responsibility too early because they are fooled into believing they have no authority to exercise it. Your children too will try to convince you of that. In fact, they have been doing it from the moment they were old enough to say "no." It's part of the sin nature in all of us that doesn't want to submit.

Those Who Plant in Tears Will Harvest with Shouts of Joy

So, if you are struggling with the willpower to go on, feeling frustrated, weary, and upset, then do what I did: go to God's Word and find solace and renewed strength to continue. I have cried many tears over my eldest son, but Psalm 126:5–6 has always given me comfort:

Those who plant in tears will harvest with shouts of joy. They weep as they go to plant their seed, but they sing as they return with the harvest. (NLT)

Don't stop planting that seed, Mom, because even though you can't yet see the fruit, as you water it with tears, God will ensure that the harvest is forthcoming. Remember, your child belongs to Him, and He loves your child even more than you do! So never, never give up on your child, especially a strong-willed child who seems to fight you every step of the way. Make sure your child has an opportunity to meet with God personally when he or she is young. It is so important

> Your child belongs to God, and He loves your child even more than you do! So never, never give up on your child.

for strong-willed children to have an encounter with God at an early age. It will give them a foundation for future surrender, something they will need to do many times in their lives as their own will tries to regain control.

Today, at sixteen, Mark is still strong-willed, but he knows when he's lost the fight. He can now back down with a grin, declaring that it was "worth a try." We have taught him the principles of win/win negotiating and the battles are much fewer and easier. He is logical, straightforward, capable of organizing anything and anyone, respectful to adults, and possesses discernment far beyond his years. Just last week, he led another one of his high school friends to the Lord and was following up with him via MSN Messenger while we were away on vacation. I believe I am only just beginning to see the harvest of the seeds of tears sown into his life, and I can assure you, I'm singing for joy!

If you have a strong-willed child into whom you have sown tear-filled seeds, don't despair: you will reap a harvest one day that will cause you to sing for joy...but never, never, never give up. God chose you to be the mother of your child—that means you have everything within you that your child needs. You are completely capable of raising your child successfully and training your child to become a champion for Jesus. You see, there is a very fine line between a leader and a rebel. Most rebels are leaders whom someone has given up on. But you can be the influence in their lives that shapes them into a world-changing leader.

Help! He's a Worrier!

Parenting the Negative Child

Chapter Two

Help! He's a Worrier!
Parenting the Negative Child

*"For God has not given us a spirit of fear, but of power
and of love and of a sound mind."*
—2 Timothy 1:7

*I*was more careful when naming my second son. Nathan
Andrew was thirteen when I discovered I was pregnant
with our third son, Benjamin. The name *Nathan* means
"a gift from God," and he truly is just that. Nathan kissed
me when he found out I was pregnant, and he began danc-
ing around me, saying, "Thank you for making me an older
brother." This was a far different reaction from the one I'd
received from his older brother! Nathan was so different from
Mark that at first I thought there was something wrong with
him! Nathan could play by himself and he didn't scream all
the time. Still, he presented challenges all his own.

I noticed something strange would happen when we went
to church or were in a crowd of people. From the moment he

was just a few days old, he would turn his head away and tuck his face into my side so that all people could see was the back of his head! His older brother, on the other hand, was much more social. On the first day of kindergarten, Mark had said to me, "You can go, Mom. This is for big boys and you can't stay!" But Nathan was proving the extreme opposite. When he was old enough to walk, he would often hide himself behind a chair, content to stay there for hours all by himself…probably trying to escape from his older brother!

We ran a church home group in our house when Nathan was about two years old. Every time guests would arrive, he would start crying. He hated people in "his" house and would act up until they left. As I was involved in leading the group, it was very difficult for me to have any input into the group with a screaming child clinging to my legs! Every week I was faced with the same dilemma. I could see that he was genuinely afraid when the house was full and noisy, and yet I found it hard not to get frustrated with him. I have felt called to the ministry since I was a little girl and I knew I was in the center of God's will, but it seemed that I was unable to be *both* the parent he needed me to be *and* the leader I wanted to be.

Stand with Your Children and Help Them Face Their Fears

One particular evening, I had to remove Nathan from the meeting. As usual, he was crying fearfully, clinging to me, and disrupting the meeting. I took him up to the bedroom, rocking him distractedly, and out of habit I shot a prayer heavenward: "God, help me! I have no idea what to do! Do I demand that he pull himself together (which was what I wanted to do!) or do I sympathize with his fear?" Like a flash, the answer came back—and as usual it was so much better than either of the options I had been toying with. I felt God say to me, "Jane, you need to *stand with him and help him face his fear.*" It suddenly dawned on me that his fear was paralyzing him, making any rational thought become irrational. I had been dismissing his fear rather than helping him to overcome it. It was very real to him. He needed the comfort of knowing that I understood his fear and the security of knowing that I would stand with him and help him to face it.

> **Stand with your children and help them face their fears.**

I took a big breath and said to him, "You are frightened because there are lots of people in your house and you don't know them." He nodded and his bottom lip began to tremble again. I continued: "Mommy understands that you are frightened. Mommy is here with you, and Jesus, who is a lot bigger and stronger than Mommy, is with you too." I prayed with him and asked Jesus to come back into the meeting with us. He calmed down and I told him, "You and Mommy and Jesus are going back into the room now." I was holding him tightly, and as we moved closer to the door he began to whimper again. I whispered into his ear that I was there and so was Jesus. We went into the room and he sat on my knee. I held him tight as I entered into the conversation in the room. Before long he wriggled out of my arms and began to engage with the person next to me. Before the end of the meeting he was walking around among the crowd. From that day on, Nathan looked forward to home group in our house.

You see, when God gave me Nathan to look after for Him, He knew the kind of life I would have to lead, He knew the demands of ministry, and He also knew the kind of personality Nathan would have. Therefore I have to conclude that all those factors are compatible rather than discordant. In other words, rather than the job that I do damaging or disadvantaging Nathan, the situations that I find myself in are opportunities for him to face challenges and to grow, to overcome giants in his own life so that one day he can teach others to do the same. He also needs me, as his mother, to help him face those challenges and not expect him to deal with them alone. He needs my strength and positive encouragement for every battle he fights. And he needs me to be there with him to celebrate the victories along the way. I tell him it's not a coincidence that his middle name, Andrew, means "manly and brave." Now, at fourteen, he can look adults in the eye and greet them with a smile. He has no trouble connecting with others, and many people have trouble believing me when I tell them how fearful he was as a small child.

He was not only fearful; he was also incredibly negative. I remember when Ashley and I tried to teach him to tie his shoelaces, ride his bike, or dress himself, and he would be in tears, saying, "I can't! I can't!" over and over again. With a big smile, we would patiently say to him, "Yes, you can! Of course you can!"

Teach Them How to Overcome, Equip Them for Future Battles

I remember one day taking Nathan for a walk down at the creek. His older brother was way ahead as usual. We were crossing the river on some stepping stones and each stone was a huge obstacle to Nathan. Finally, he refused to go any further and stood crying and saying, "I can't!"

I stood with him and said, "Yes, you can! Say, 'I can!'"

"I can't!"

"Say, 'I can!'"

"I can't!"

"Yes, you can! Just say it. You don't have to do it, just say it."

"I can't!"

"That's it! You nearly said it!"

"I can't!" He was half laughing and half crying now.

"I can! I can! I can! I can!" I began to chant in a little song.

He stopped crying and laughed a little. Before long he started to say, "I can! I can!" And he began to sing my silly little song with me. Then, without warning, his feet began to get the message and he jumped each rock like it was a tall building, his face shining with pride as his little legs mastered those stones.

> Negative children need you to pull them out of their negativity, and the best way to do that is to get them to laugh.

Negative Children Need Distraction from the Paralysis of Fear

Negative children need distraction from the paralysis of fear that keeps them fettered to the "I can'ts" of life. They need *you* to pull them out of their negativity, and the best way to do that is to distract them and get them to laugh. Nathan has learned to laugh at his own negativity now, and I've taught him to see its advantages. He sees the problems all the time, but that also means he gets a head start on working out the solutions to those problems. Likewise, if *your* negative child sees the problems before anyone else does, teach him to solve the problems before anyone else.

Nathan will often say, "We can't because…" He'll give us twelve reasons why we can't. Rather than dismiss his assessment, I ask him to find a way that we can. He often comes up with amazing insights and has problem-solving skills that

> **Equip your children for future battles by teaching them how to overcome today.**

neither I nor his brother possess. He was brilliant at the computer game "Lemmings" when he was younger. Long after the rest of us had given up, he would sit for hours trying different approaches to save the little creatures.

Parenting Nathan was (and still is!) an interesting challenge for me. I am a naturally positive person and have struggled to understand his persistent negativity. One thing I haven't wanted to do, though, is to make him feel he has to be like me, or like his older brother. I have been careful to encourage the great strengths that he possesses, such as kindness and generosity. I don't want him to feel like his negativity is a handicap. Rather, I have taught him that it can be a powerful tool if used correctly. I am so proud of the giants he has tackled at such a young age. It doesn't mean they won't ever raise their ugly heads again; it just means that we are laying a foundation in his life that is teaching him how to overcome and will equip him for future battles.

Unfortunately, negative children seem to be born with a whine in their mouth! From the moment he could make himself understood, rather than demand things like his older brother, Nathan would whine for them. There are few things less tolerable than a child who does not stop whining, and Nathan was one of the best!

One particular day, after listening to him whining non-stop for most of the morning, I said to him, "Come here, Nathan. Now open your mouth." He opened his mouth, wondering what on earth I was doing. I reached into his mouth and, with a face that was screwed up in disgust, I said, "I'm taking this yucky whine out of your mouth and I'm putting it in the garbage." We walked over to the garbage can and I put the "whine" in. He looked at the garbage can and then looked at me and I said, "That's the end of the whining." It worked—for a while! But after that, every time he began to whine, I would say, "Open your mouth!" and I would make a big deal trying to find the whine. Sometimes it was tricky…it could be hiding under his tongue; at other times I was sure he had swallowed it. But it became a ritual between us that would bring attention to the fact that he needed to change the way he was communicating. It also broke the tension and usually had the desired effect of breaking his negative mind-set for long enough to have a little peace. At fourteen, it no longer works, of course, but sometimes I still threaten to do it!

"I Will Try to Control Every Negative Thought before It Becomes a Word"

Just recently, after one of our "talks," Nathan wrote this statement on a piece of paper as a reminder to himself: "I will try to control every negative thought before it becomes a word." There are precious moments when I look at him and realize he has done just that. Often, when he has a negative attitude about something, he will be silent for a moment, and then he will turn his whole attitude around with one positive statement. It doesn't happen all the time, but the fact that it happens at all in the life of a fourteen-year-old boy is a triumph to celebrate. I tell him I am so proud of him as I know thirty-year-olds who still need to learn that skill!

"What Was Your Day at School Like?"

It is so like Nathan to think of the details I had forgotten! It's true, he does need his space. Because he does not have a need to be excessively social, for him just going to school each day is generally enough people contact for one day. Often he will get home from school and quietly walk into his room and shut the door. Now, being a people person myself, I initially thought that this behavior signaled some strange depression or serious withdrawal. When he first started doing it, I would make a point of following him into his room and going through the "million questions" routine. "Are you alright?" "What was your day at school like?" "Did anyone hurt you?" "Did you get in trouble?" "Do you need to talk about something?"

He gave me a big sigh one day and said, "No, Mom! I don't want you to get upset, but I just don't want to talk to anyone at the moment. Everything is fine, I just need some space." "Oh," I said a little sheepishly as I backed out the door, wondering what it was like to "need space." The truth is, I didn't even know how much "space" to give him. I asked my husband, who is an expert on "space," and he gave me the wisdom I will share with you. He said, "He does need space; leave him for about an hour. He may come out by himself after that if he's ready. But if he doesn't, go in and gently say to him that he has had his space and that now he must connect with the rest of the family and not continue to isolate himself."

It was great wisdom that I had to pass on to his older brother, who also doesn't understand the concept of needing "space." I should have known; even as a very small boy Nathan would play for hours in his room with his Legos. I would often go in and get on my stomach on the floor with him and join in his battlefield, or whatever it was he had constructed. He would look at me with a pained expression and say, "Mom, you are not in this game. You can't just walk in. The story doesn't have room for you in it." Ouch! I take care, though, to make sure that after he has had his "space," he knows that he must come out and interact with others, as too much "space" is not healthy for a child of his temperament.

> Negative children need space, but too much space is not healthy for children of this temperament.

It Is Important to Give Your Children Choices

Yesterday I asked Nathan what I should tell all the other mothers who might read this book about how they should treat their own children who may have a personality similar to his. This was his priceless wisdom:

"Tell them we need our space, and tell them to give us choices to make; they don't have to be the big things, but let us decide some of the smaller things."

Now, I'm not saying that you need to ask them what they want to eat for every meal, what they want to wear, or where they'd like to go. I have seen some mothers do this, and they are only making a rod for their own back. Nevertheless, there are times when, within certain boundaries, there is room to give your child a choice. The choice may be as simple as "Do you want us to go to the shops before lunch or would you prefer we go after lunch?" or "We need to get dressed for dinner; will you be wearing your blue jeans or your new shorts?" Either one would be acceptable, but rather than tell them what you want them to wear, give them a choice between a few things that would all be suitable. It is far easier than trying to get them to take something off that they now have their heart set on wearing! Occasionally, if Nathan has had a bad day at school, I will say, "Let's go out for dinner tonight, and, Nathan, you get to choose where we go." It's almost always the worst junk food you can buy. But it's worth putting up with a greasy burger when you see the gratitude on his face that expresses, "Thanks for noticing and caring, Mom."

Help! They're All Different!

Understand That Each Child Is Special

Chapter Three

Help! They're All Different!
Understand That Each Child Is Special

*"Everyone has a talent. What is rare is
the courage to nurture it…"*
— Erica Jong

The New Arrival

Benjamin arrived by Caesarian section on April 17, 2003. Physically he is a carbon copy of his oldest brother, Mark. Yet, unlike Mark, he is peace-loving and con-genial. (Thank You, Jesus!) Like Mark, he too has proven to be allergic to milk products and, thanks to our past experience, we discovered his allergies early! As I'm writing this, he is recovering from an ear infection for which we had to give him antibiotics—antibiotics, we now know, he's allergic to!

I am constantly entranced by Benjamin's distinctive quali-ties. He already has a wicked sense of humor and a propensity toward the dramatic, a flair he shares with Nathan. He also has a magnetic personality. People stop me all the time, not to talk to me, but to him! I'm writing this from a hotel in the north of Borneo, enjoying a long-awaited "long service leave." The hotel is filled with Japanese tourists. This morning in the pool, the normally shy Japanese were crowding around Benjamin and me in the pool, cooing and laughing at him, totally oblivious to my presence. Later they all lined up to have their photo taken with him. I love it! In fact, it has happened so often this week that if you are ever in Japan and have the opportunity to look through a photo album, there is a good chance you will see a photo of my baby in there!

> **There is something special about your children and God wants you to help them find out what it is.**

He is a delight to the entire family and, of course, if I could turn back time, I wouldn't alter a thing! Already, he is a worshipper. As soon as we get into the car he will ask for music to be turned on, and he won't give up until we switch it on. I often glance in the rear vision mirror to see him with one hand raised, lost in baby songs to Jesus. When we drive into church on Sundays we usually arrive in time for the music rehearsal, which we can hear from the parking lot. He will look at me with his face shining and every part of his little body moves to the beat. The rest of the story about Benjamin is yet unwritten, but I'm sure he will continue to provide me with enough material for another book!

God Wants to Help You Discover Your Children's Special Gifts

There is something special about my three boys, but that doesn't surprise me. Neither do I apologize for bragging to you about them, because there is something special about each child God has entrusted to my care. There is something special about your children too, and God wants you to help them find out what it is.

While both my older boys are strong leaders, they are radically different. Nathan doesn't like the same clothes as his brother; neither does he have the same haircut or play the same sport or the same musical instrument. He is very much his own person, unique and gifted. He's a dreamer and he's kind, artistic, generous, and musical. Mark is strong, decisive, and dependable in a crisis.

Each of my children is distinctly different and strongly individual. I'm sure yours are too! As a mother I feel challenged by this; challenged because, as individuals, they need to be treated with respect, challenged to make sure I understand each of them well. I'm constantly seeking to get to know them better. I need to know their strengths so that I can encourage them and sharpen them. I also need to understand their weaknesses so that I can build strength into each weakness and train the boys to overcome them.

One of the ways I have done this is to teach my boys about the various temperaments and personalities people possess. I want them not only to understand themselves better, but to understand each other too.

Identify Their Personality Temperaments and Champion Their Strengths

Over the years my mother has given me books for the boys and many of them have turned out to be incredible tools to help navigate some of the territory necessary for success. One of them was a book called *The Treasure Tree* by John Trent and

Gary Smalley, published by Thomas Nelson. In a delightful children's story, it outlines the four different personality temperaments and champions their strengths. Reading it with the boys gave rise to some wonderful discussions on uniqueness and brought a new appreciation for their own capabilities.

I will never forget going into Mark's classroom when he was in second grade and seeing the words "Self-control" in big letters stuck to his desk. I was quite taken aback and was ready to confront the teacher until I noticed that all the desks had words on them. Some had "Patience," others had "Kindness" and "Humility." Seeing my consternation, the teacher came up to me and began to explain why the words were there and what they meant. She said that at the beginning of the year she had helped each of the children identify a personal weakness that, if they worked on that weakness, would benefit not only them but the rest of the class as well. I glanced back down at Mark's desk. "Self-control." I couldn't argue; she had it right: it was his biggest weakness. His lack of it made him call out in class, made him get out of his seat when he was supposed to be sitting still, and made him lash out at anyone who gave him a hard time. What a simple yet brilliant idea!

I went home and decided that each year I would do that for the boys. I would sit down with them and discuss what areas they felt they needed to grow in, and we would present it as a "challenge goal" each year. It wasn't done formally; we just spoke about it. Then, whenever they displayed the character trait they had identified, I would encourage them in it. Whenever an opportunity presented itself for them to develop that trait I would remind them of their goal. Mark identified self-control as his challenge nearly every year until seventh grade! We spent many "bedroom times" talking about this trait. I would say to him, "If you can't control yourself, then I will have to do it...it's your choice!" There were many times when I wondered whether I was getting through or not. Now that he is a teenager, I believe a lack of self-control is no longer the giant in his life that it used to be. In fact, there are many times when I am encouraged by the amount of self-control he displays, especially when his younger brother is an expert at testing it!

With Nathan, I have worked on his desire for vengeance. I remember one incident when he was barely two years of age. His brother had a plastic golf set, and one day he was swinging one of the clubs wildly around his head when he accidentally hit Nathan in the head. I made Mark put the club down and apologize. I then comforted Nathan, who eventually stopped crying. As soon as he got down off my knee, he went straight to the golf club, took it in his hand,

> Sit down with your children, discuss areas they feel they need to grow in, and regularly encourage them.

and slammed it over his brother's head as he was playing on the floor. I looked at Nathan and thought, "Okay, we have a real issue with revenge here." To this day, he always wants to get even and will scheme ways to get back at those who have hurt him. We have spoken about it over and over again, and the hardest thing for him is to let an offense go without reprisal. He is learning to do it and I am proud of him.

One of the mistakes I made early on in my parenting was to communicate the same way to both of the older boys. Now Mark, as you have heard, is very loud and strong. When he argues, he does so with all his energy and passion. It takes an equally strong response from me to even get through to him. If he feels you are somehow not as passionate or strong about your opinion, he will steamroll you relentlessly. You have to match fire with fire with him, and make sure you have your wits about you, as he will argue every possible angle. He does know when he has lost, though. It is usually at the point when your passion matches his that he concedes defeat. Sometimes he has been known to say, "Why didn't you tell me before that you felt so strongly about that?" He seems to be the kind of child who only understands a strong response to his strong challenge.

> Children are unique: we need to communicate differently with each of them. The rules are the same, but the method needs to change.

Nathan, on the other hand, is far more sensitive. I found this out the hard way. One day when he was about three, I began to speak sternly to him in a loud, clear voice, correcting him for something he had done wrong. When he didn't respond, I increased my volume! Eventually he put his little hands up to his ears and his bottom lip started to tremble. He still didn't say anything, but I thought to myself, "My goodness, what am I doing to this child?" I took him in my arms and told him I loved him. I realized from that day on that he needed a completely different approach. When I raise my voice with him, rather than "getting through" to him, I am actually shutting him down!

The boys are so unique that I need to communicate differently with each of them. If I want to make myself heard and understood I need to learn the emotional language they speak. You see, the rules are the same; it's just the method that needs to change.

Being "Different" Is Not Wrong; It's Just "Different"

The other thing my boys have had to learn is that being "different" is not wrong; it's just "different." I remember one particularly frustrating time when the two older boys had been fighting and putting each other down all day. I had endured about all I could take, so I called "time out" and sat them down. I began to talk to them about the fact that they were on the same team. Yes, they were like the players on a basketball team. Each player plays in a different position on the court; some are good at defense, and others are skilled at offense. It takes all different kinds of players to play on the same team, but if the players don't play together and understand each other's strengths, they will fail miserably.

I told the boys that if they were playing a game of basketball and they started to attack one of their own players, even if the coach didn't pull them out of the game, it would still hurt the team. In attacking their own teammate they are actually attacking themselves. They are damaging their own potential to be a winner. It's the same in a family. We are all on the same team, even though we all have different strengths and abilities. Just because someone doesn't have the same strengths you have does not mean you can ridicule or attack him or her. It merely means that he or she will be able to contribute something to the team that you lack. If we value one another and the unique contributions that we can each make to the family, we will have a new level of understanding regarding how a family should operate.

We were doing some paving outside our house one day. Ashley had rented a roller to flatten the sand before the pavers went down. Ashley was called away and I decided to try to continue on without him...I wanted to surprise him when he got back. Now, the roller had been left at the front of the driveway and I was working up a sweat trying with sheer brute force to get it over the stones and up the driveway. My eldest son came out and lent his strength to mine, but we still couldn't budge it. Nathan wandered out and watched us for a few moments. Then he walked up to us and said, "Come here!" He grabbed the handle, swung it over the other way, and instead of pushing, he began to pull it in a rocking motion. He pulled it up the driveway in no time! My eldest son and I looked at each other incredulously and followed him up the driveway. We gained a new respect for Nathan from that day on, and he felt special because he was able to contribute something that no one else had been able to do.

> Discover your special gifts now. You will struggle to see greatness in your children if no one has seen it in you.

We All Have Something of Value to Contribute to Our World

The ability to see uniqueness in others comes from the knowledge that we are all unique, that God has created us all with great diversity and value, and that we all have something of value to contribute to our world. There is also something special about you, Mom. Perhaps when you were a child, no one took the time to discover your special gift. Perhaps now as an adult you are still wondering what your gift is. It is never too late to discover it. God is your Father now, so ask Him to help you discover what it is and together enjoy the gift He has placed within you.

It is important to discover your special gifts now. You will struggle to see greatness in your children if no one has seen it in you. Often we see parents who desire to see their own undiscovered greatness surface in their children. So many parents want their children to be able to do the things they longed to do as a child, but no one took the time to develop the talents within them. There are too many frustrated piano players trying to make a maestro out of their child. There are too many undiscovered football talents urging their children on to sporting success to fulfill their own dreams of greatness. Each child is unique and has gifts and talents that may be vastly different from yours. Each is a special package waiting to be discovered by you—the parent—and used by God.

Help! I've Lost My Confidence!

Don't Throw Away Your Confidence: Stand Still and the Lord Will Fight for You!

Help! I've Lost My Confidence!

Don't Throw Away Your Confidence: Stand Still and the Lord Will Fight for You!

Somebody said that it couldn't be done,
But he with a chuckle replied
That "maybe it couldn't," but he would be one
Who wouldn't say so till he'd tried.
So he buckled right in with the trace of a grin
On his face. If he worried he hid it.
He started to sing as he tackled the thing
That couldn't be done, and he did it.

—Edgar A. Guest (from "It Couldn't Be Done")

*T*here are many times when, as a mother, I feel inadequate and ill-equipped, or I just plain have no idea what to do next. Nevertheless, I am confident that God thinks I have what it takes to look after the three precious gifts He has given me; to shape, teach, and then release them to be the champions and men of God they were born to be. Think about this for a moment: before the foundations of the world, your children were in God's heart, and when it was time for them to enter the world, He scanned the earth looking for the best mother he could find. He was looking for the mother who would have all the right things inside her for that special child; the mother who would nurture and love the child, training and protecting him in order to realize the potential that He placed within him. His eyes stopped when they fell on you. He had just found the best mother in the whole world for that child—*you!*

> **When your child was born, God gave you the heavenly mandate to develop that child into all that He has destined your child to be.**

When your child was born, God gave you the heavenly mandate to develop that child into all that He has destined your child to be. And yet He didn't leave you to do it alone, without any direction or guidance. He promised that He would never leave you or forsake you. Others might, but He never will! This means that when you feel weak, when you feel like you have blown it, or when you feel you simply have no strength left, all you need to do is call Him and He will answer. God has promised:

Call to me and I will answer you and tell you great and unsearchable things you do not know. (Jeremiah 33:3 NIV)

What a resource! There are many times when I haven't known what to do and have felt at a loss as to where to go from here. Every time I have called out I have received an answer. It may not have been the answer I was wishing or hoping for, but it always turned out to be the best one I could hear.

I am always inspired by Genesis 18:17–19:

And the Lord said, Shall I hide from Abraham that thing which I do; seeing that Abraham shall surely become a great and mighty nation, and all the nations of the earth shall be blessed in him? **For I know him**, *that he will command his children and his household after him, and they shall keep the way of the* LORD, *to do justice and judgment; that the* LORD *may bring upon Abraham that which he hath spoken of him.* (KJV)

God didn't hold anything back from Abraham because *He knew him* and knew that he would teach his children to keep God's laws! I want Him to say that about me too! I have a mandate from God to parent my children. God believes that I can do it—so I am determined to do so with confidence!

Your Children Have Seeds of Greatness Placed within Them

If you are a mother, you have the same mandate. You have the same access to the resources you will need to fulfill that mandate. Sometimes the answers to questions may lie hidden, but this just serves to entice us back into the arms of the One who made us. It maintains the link of dependence so that we don't stray too far from the blueprint in God's heart for our children. So, Mom, don't ever think you don't have what it takes. Don't be tempted to give up. Your children have seeds of greatness placed within them, planted by God before the foundations of the world were laid. He chose *you* to water, nurture, and bring them into the light…it's *your* mandate from God. If ever there was a reason to be confident as a parent it is this: God knows you've got what it takes! So don't allow the challenges of parenthood to undermine your confidence.

In Hebrews 10:35 we find this instruction:

So do not throw away your confidence; it will be richly rewarded. (NIV)

Alternatively, this verse might be translated:

Do not, therefore, fling away your fearless confidence, for it carries a great and glorious compensation of reward. (AMP)

Have you ever seen two boxers facing each other in the ring before a fight? They stare into each other's eyes to see who will drop his gaze first. They gesture in an intimidating way; exaggerating their own confidence in an attempt to bluff their opponent into throwing away his. It's all about confidence. They are trying to break down their opponent's confidence so they will have the upper hand.

You too have an enemy who is trying to get you to throw away your confidence. He is attempting to stare you down, seeking to intimidate you and convince you that you are not going to succeed. He is whispering to you that you are going to fail as a parent, or maybe that you already have. He wants you to give up in despair and declare that the battle is all but lost. You must realize that Satan's words only have credence if you allow them to. He is trying to trick you into doubting your mandate and questioning whether you can be successful as a parent. He is staring you down to try to make you throw away your confidence.

The verse in Hebrews doesn't say, "Be careful—someone might steal your confidence or take it away from you!" Rather, it says that *you* should not *throw away* your confidence. Satan cannot actually touch your confidence; he can only fool you into thinking that you don't have what it takes. The only way you can lose your confidence is if you relinquish it. The only way you can lose it is if you loosen you grip on it!

It seems that we so easily become intimidated, unsettled, and discouraged to the point at which we throw away the confidence that we can shape the children God has given us into the adults He intends them to become. Today, more than ever, parenting demands confidence. As a mother, you need confidence based not in your own abilities, but in the knowledge that God searched the entire planet for the best mother for your child and chose you! This must be a fundamental conviction deep within your heart. Don't throw away your confidence. If you feel your grip loosening, then tighten it again because, as is promised in Hebrews, your confidence will be "richly rewarded."

> Satan can't touch your confidence; he can only fool you into thinking that you don't have what it takes.

The Confident Ones Seem to Get the Breaks

Have you noticed that it is always the confident ones who seem to get the breaks? That is not coincidence; it is a reward! I recall going to the cinema with my parents and my older sister when I was about four years old. During the intermission someone would come out to entertain the audience while they changed reels (boy, that's showing my age!). On this particular occasion, a gentleman came out with a chocolate bar in his hand and waved it before us asking, "Who wants this?"

My hand must have been the first one up—I have always loved anything edible! He went on to announce, "If you come up here on stage and do the twist, you can have the chocolate."

I really wanted the chocolate, but I wasn't sure if I had enough confidence to go up on stage and do the twist. While I was still contemplating what to do, my older sister jumped from her seat, ran to the front, climbed the steps to the stage, and did the twist. She was rewarded with the chocolate and a burst of applause from the audience who, like me, wished they had the confidence to do what she did. It was simple; she had the confidence, so she got the reward. I may have wanted the prize, and although I could have done what was being asked, I missed out on the reward because I didn't have confidence.

> "Confidence pays you wages." Wages help you live... They pay for your dream.

The original Greek for *"confidence has a reward"* can also be translated as "confidence pays you wages." It is worth reflecting on this translation. What do wages do? They help you live. They pay for your dream. They create an investment for your future. Wages are a source of supply for life. As parents, we need a ready supply of wisdom, authority, patience, perception, creativity, and faith. God makes them available to us—and more. Indeed, these are the "wages" of the confident parent—the parent who understands that the resources come from God, not themselves, and that they are freely accessible.

Confident parents do not simply draw on confidence in themselves or their abilities and talents. Neither do they need to "talk themselves up." The confidence they rely on is not merely a subjective feeling of being in control and able to "make it." Rather, to be confident parents, we must understand that God is bigger than our circumstances. He wants the best for us and is capable of fulfilling every promise He has made to us. When we understand that God is all-powerful and that nothing is too hard for Him, we find confidence that enables us to draw on God's resources and overcome our weaknesses and failings as parents.

Throwing Away Your Confidence Limits the Potential of the Next Generation

Satan wants you to throw away your confidence in your ability to parent so that you are robbed of its reward. He wants to reduce your wages—to cut you off from accessing your source of supply. If he can cause you to discard your confidence, he can undermine your authority as a parent and the mandate you have from God. Without a doubt, this will affect your children. Fooling you into throwing away your confidence is Satan's way of messing with the finished product. It's his way of limiting the potential of the next generation.

Our confidence as parents must be able to withstand being tested because—believe me—parenting tests your confidence over and over again! Think about a test at school. First, the teacher diligently coaches you, providing all the knowledge and material you need to pass the test. When the appointed time comes, you must take the test. You take your place at your desk. You are surrounded by your friends, but they cannot help you. You are, essentially, on your own. The test is not to find out how much the teacher knows, but to assess what you have learned. If, despite the pressure of the test conditions, you are able to produce the correct answers, you pass and can move on to more advanced, stimulating, and challenging material. Of course, you can pretend you're sick, or just not show up, but if you do, you will never pass the test. Consequently, you will not be able to move on to anything new, but will repeat the same material again and again until you pass the test.

In parenting, tests may consist of self-doubt, unfavorable circumstances, or weariness that tempts us to give in. Similarly, our wisdom, understanding, and patience will be tested as our children grow and develop, emerging as increasingly independent individuals who are eager to push boundaries. You can pretend it's not happening, but you won't pass the test. The only way to pass is to accept the tests and to face them, relying on God's Word rather than feelings, remaining in relationship with Him, and drawing on the resources He makes available.

> The Israelites threw away their confidence and ended up wandering in the wilderness for forty years.

In the Old Testament, the Israelites experienced a test of their confidence after God led them out of captivity in Egypt. They failed their test because they only had a confidence based on circumstances. When things around them seemed unfavorable, they doubted God's ability to be strong on their behalf or to provide what they needed. As a consequence, they threw away their confidence and ended up wandering in the wilderness for forty years. Satan doesn't mind if we stumble around without any confidence because he knows that we won't be going anywhere. He doesn't even mind us having the confidence that is circumstance-driven, because he can manipulate that with adverse circumstances. On the other hand, he is frightened when we begin to build a confidence deep within our spirit that is not dependent on circumstances, but on God. He is terrified of what happens when parents hold confidently to the mandate God has given them for their children.

The result of passing tests is that we develop a deep sense of confidence in God and His purpose for our lives as an intrinsic character trait. The consequence is a steadiness and purposefulness in life that is not swayed by feelings or circumstances. Difficult times will arise, negative emotions will be experienced, but our confidence need not diminish.

In Exodus 14, the Israelites had been slaves in Egypt for 430 years. Finally Pharaoh let them go. They were heading out of Egypt, loaded up with wealth and possessions given to them by their Egyptian neighbors. They were about to commence a new era of freedom and liberty, filled with purpose and hope for the future. The Bible describes them as "marching out boldly." That's exactly how some of us start out as new parents, loaded up with the promises of God and the great expectations we have for our kids.

The Israelites began their journey confident in God's ability to look after them. Their heads were held high, and they were full of boldness and confidence. God spoke to them, giving them specific directions regarding where to go and what to do. They followed His directions, but this just seemed to lead them into greater trouble. Have you ever felt like that? You faithfully keep doing the right things in your parenting, but things don't seem to get any better.

Satan Does Not Want You to Step Out with Instructions for a New Generation

The Israelites reached as far as the Red Sea and camped where God had commanded them, but it appeared that the enemy had them cornered. Pharaoh sought to enslave them again. He didn't want them to break free and begin a new life, a new culture. Similarly, Satan does not want you to step out with a mandate from God or with instructions for a new generation. Because of this, he will try to knock your confidence. You see, once the Israelites crossed the Red Sea, they had gone past the point of no return. Satan doesn't want us to go past the point of no return on our journey as parents. He wants you to remain under his influence and intimidation, and the only way he can do that is to get you to throw away your confidence.

> Satan wants you to remain under his influence and intimidation and the only way he can do that is to get you to throw away your confidence.

In Exodus 14:8, the Israelites were marching out boldly. Two verses later, it says they were terrified! Somewhere between verses eight and ten they had thrown away their confidence. Likewise, somewhere after launching out as parents we are tempted to throw our confidence away, to throw our hands in the air, and say, "I give up! I don't know what went wrong!"

I love the response Moses gave the people. It's the same one you need to hear right now:

Do not be afraid. Stand firm and you will see the deliverance the LORD will bring you today. The Egyptians you see today you will never see again. The LORD will fight for you; you need only to be still. (Exodus 14:13–14 NIV)

God knew what He was doing when He led them to that place. He intended that their enemy, who had enslaved them for generations, should be defeated once and for all. That is exactly what happened when Moses led the people across the Red Sea.

God wants to do the same for you. He wants you to experience a new culture in your life, a culture of freedom and purpose, a culture of confidence in your parenting. Some of you feel like the enemy has come and hemmed you in and the confidence you had is beginning to slide. Satan has come against your confidence, against your relationship with your children, and he's been telling you that you will never make it…that you have started over so many times before and failed, and this will be no different.

Not Everyone Feels Confident, but Everyone Can Make a Decision to Be Confident

Not everyone feels confident, but everyone can make a decision to be confident. There are many times when I don't *feel* confident as a parent. I ask myself, "Have I just made the right decision? Am I doing the right thing?"

It is at these times that I come back to the truth that I am God's choice to be my children's mother. I have what it takes. He has every resource I need to be a confident parent. So, although I may not feel confident, I choose to persist, to draw on God's wisdom, and to parent with conviction. I choose to stand still and allow the Lord to fight with me. This is what defines the confident parent. Whatever your challenges as a parent, God has called you to the task. He has every resource you need too. So stand still and be a confident parent, for God is right there alongside you fighting for your children.

What Do You See?

Choose to See in
Your Children
What God Sees

Chapter Five

What Do You See?
*Choose to See in Your Children
What God Sees*

*"It takes little talent to see clearly what lies
under one's nose, a good deal of it to know in
which direction to point that organ."
—W.H. Auden*

Y ou are so lazy!"

I am ashamed to say that these are words I have spoken myself, personal words that wound and go deep into a child's spirit. These words should never leave the mouth of a mother. You see, when I spoke these words, I was looking at the wrong thing. I was looking at the negative qualities of a child who has so many other positive qualities. I try not to speak that way now. I have determined not to criticize and pull down, no matter how frustrated I am! It's not easy to see the positives when the negatives seem to scream at you so loudly. It's not easy to see a child who is creative when all you see is crayon all over the wall. It's not easy to see a child who is a leader when all you hear is confrontation. It's not easy to see persistence when all you see is stubbornness.

What you focus on is so important. There are already too many people focusing on your child's negative qualities: "Johnny, you are always talking! Johnny, sit still! Johnny, you will never get ahead if you don't learn to listen! Johnny, you are impossible!" They hear this all day with very few encouraging words in between. Constant negativity eats away at their emotional reserves, emptying their tank. They arrive home to the place that should be a safe haven, a place that should be the filling station for those empty tanks. And yet sometimes they hear it all over again!

> If you don't build up and encourage your child, who will? Your children rely on you to fill their confidence reservoir.

If you don't build up and encourage your children, let's face it—who will? Perhaps they may be fortunate enough to have one or two teachers in the entire school life who may say something positive to them, but that is like trying to fill a reservoir with a cup! Your children rely on you to fill their reservoir. The secret is to change what you see, to choose to focus on the good. It's there somewhere! Sometimes you just have to look harder!

Moses' Mother Chose to See the Good in Her Son

I am so inspired by the story of Moses' mother. It is a story of hope and courage, a story of triumph, a story of one mother, a woman whose name we don't even know, who rescued her own child from genocide. He grew to become one of the greatest leaders the world has ever known—all because she chose to see the good. In Exodus 2:1-2 we read these simple words:

> *A man of the house of Levi went and took as wife a daughter of Levi. So the woman conceived and bore a son. And when she saw that he was a beautiful child, she hid him three months.*

She saw how beautiful he was! Now this might not seem unusual to you. I'm sure every mother looks at her baby and thinks that he or she is the best-looking and most beautiful baby she has ever seen, even when we all know that some of them are downright ugly!

When my babies were born I can remember thinking that they were the best-looking babies in the whole world. In fact, when Mark was just a few months old I sent a photo of him to a baby competition and was absolutely convinced he would win. I laugh now when I look at it. He looked like a cross between Pierce Brosnan and a monkey. But I thought he was gorgeous then. Today, of course, he really is gorgeous—honestly!

See beyond the Physical Attributes

Now I'm not talking just about the physical appearance of your children. I'm talking about seeing beyond that. What do you *see* when you look at your children?

Do you see a leader? Or do you see a noisy, demanding child who is always bullying those around him?

> **Do you see someone who has a gentle spirit, who can care for the weak?** Or do you see a whining, emotionally liable child who is exhausting to parent?
>
> **Do you see a strategist?** Or do you see a child who is manipulative and deceptive?
>
> **Do you see a negotiator?** Or do you see someone who wears you down so that you eventually give in?

> Once you see their positive qualities, pray them into and over their lives.

Once You See Their Positive Qualities, You Have Something to Work With

Once you have seen something, you have something to work with. You are not just working with manners and behavior, you are working with character and you are molding their spirit. When you have seen something in your child, it will help you in those times when you cry yourself to sleep at night; it will help you in those times when you worry yourself sick because of his or her attitude. If you have seen something, you can keep that special quality firmly in your focus. You can pray it into and over their lives. You can speak to the positive qualities in them, even when they are only displaying the negative. Don't just look at the surface, don't just see the negative, or you could end up being quite misled.

A Mother in Disguise

A funny thing happened three days after I had Benjamin by Caesarian section. During that time our church was hosting a major Easter production. Many of my good friends were involved in the production and they had spent hours and hours building the set and rehearsing. I really wanted to be there even though everyone was telling me to "just get the video." That's like telling a guy who has the opportunity to go to the Australian Soccer League grand final, "Don't bother! Just get the video!" There's nothing like being there; the atmosphere is amazing!

Being sanguine, I really didn't want to miss out. I knew if I turned up at the church I would be mobbed by our well-meaning congregation who had shared every moment of this pregnancy with me. I needed a disguise. I thought about going in a wheelchair as an old lady, but knew that the more astute members wouldn't be fooled. So I rang my personal assistant and asked her to hire me a costume from the costume shop. My sister, who had traveled from interstate, came to the hospital, and I told the nursing staff that I was going on leave for the night. (It never pays to ask...they might have said no!)

We reached the car and I changed into my costume: a black, full-length, full-faced burka! The only thing showing through were the whites of my eyes, and I had even gone to the trouble of wearing extra-heavy eyeliner! We approached the church in a slow shuffle, which suited my Caesarian scar nicely and helped with the disguise. I entered the foyer and, to their credit, people didn't stare or make me feel uncomfortable. I was shown to a seat the head usher had saved for me. She was the only other person who knew about the prank, apart from my husband, who disowned me for the night. He couldn't believe I would do such a thing, and kept glancing in my direction, shaking his head.

I must admit that I really enjoyed myself, watching people who had no idea it was I. You get a whole new look at people when their guard is down and they have no idea who you are. People came up to greet me and, of course, to complete the disguise, I spoke in a Middle Eastern accent the whole night. My cover was nearly blown, however, when Sunil, one of our wonderful board members of Indian and Muslim origin, spotted me in the crowd. He was assisting with the offering collection that night, in the section where I was seated. I could see that he was working out a way to approach me, and each time he tried, I lowered my head to speak the language he would have understood, saying, "Stay away from me, please." He respectfully complied, but I could see that he was already interceding for my soul. The evangelist in him was finding it hard to stay away.

I left the auditorium just before the altar call, and saw so many downcast faces, his included, covering me in prayer as I left. I was so proud of our church that day. They had passed a test that I never even intended for them to take. On my way to the car, my sons came running after me, half in awe that I would actually do such a thing and half bemused, wondering what I would do next!

The church still doesn't know that the incongruous visitor that night was none other than their senior pastor's wife. I'll tell them one day, and talk to them about the fact that things are not always what they seem. What we see on the outside often doesn't tell us a lot about what's happening on the inside. It is the same with our children.

Don't Judge the Outward Appearance

So many times we judge the outward appearance. The mouth says one thing, but the heart of our child is crying out to be loved. Even the most rebellious of children, the roughest street kids, just need to be loved. They just need someone to love them even when they do the wrong thing, to love them when they look different to everyone else, to love them when they know themselves that they are being unlovely. As a parent, it is too easy to get drawn into the fight. Determine the things that are important to you and only fight the battles that are worth winning. Let the rest go.

I am determined not to fight against things that will not affect my children's future success, even if it means others will look at my children and judge me as an unsuccessful mother. Sometimes what they choose to wear to church makes me shudder, but at least they want to go! They may look like they have crawled out of bed in their clothes. They may insist on wearing a baseball cap or not combing their hair. But they are in church twice every Sunday. I measure that as success. It's more important than ensuring my children wear clothes that will make me feel better when they come and talk to me in church!

> So many times we judge the outward appearance. The mouth says one thing, but the heart of our child is crying out to be loved.

What do you see in your children? It's not too late to ask God to show you your children's positive qualities. Ask Him to give you a glimpse of what He sees when He looks at them. Ask Him to give you a glimpse of their potential so that you can encourage that potential in them.

Moses' Mother Protected Him

The next thing Moses' mother did was to hide him. She hid him to *protect* him. When God gives you something, you have to protect it. This world is after your child. Pornography is everywhere, drugs can be purchased at school, and it appears that today it's no longer a question of *if* most people will have sex before marriage, just *when*. There are influences that are trying to kill the potential in your child's spirit before it even gets a chance to flourish. Protect your children: hide them, not from the world, but from the influences in the world that are negative and want to destroy the potential in your child's spirit.

Protecting your children sometimes means stopping them from going to places that are not going to be good for them. It means putting boundaries in place and limiting their activities. One night one of my boys really wanted to go to the local shopping mall to hang out with his friends. He had been asking and asking me to take him. Now, I don't like groups of kids simply hanging around shopping malls. They invariably get up to no good. I felt that my son shouldn't go, and I told him so. He argued back and forth (as they do!), wanting a good reason why he wasn't allowed to go. So I gave him one: "I just don't feel right about you going, so you're not going." Why is it that a perfectly good reason to you just doesn't seem to cut it with them? Anyway, I told him that was the end of the conversation, and he realized he had lost.

> There are influences trying to kill the potential in your child's spirit before it gets a chance to flourish. Protect your children from them.

Later that evening, we were watching the news together in the family room, and the breaking news declared: "A boy was stabbed at a local shopping mall when a gang of youths went on a rampage!" It was one of those moments when you know you don't have to say anything. A look is all that's needed. But I made sure it was a good one! The silence in the room was enough for me to feel triumphant that my "weak reason" had just been validated.

Imagine Moses, as a baby, not being able to be taken outside the home. His mother would not even have been able to have him in the main room of the house. His life would have been restricted to perhaps a small storeroom out back where he would have been kept hidden from the soldiers who came checking. In order to protect him, he was restricted. Just like Moses' mother, we also restrict our children in physical ways from playing in dangerous environments, such as busy streets, because they could get killed. (We put up fences and we shut gates.) Or we stop them from touching power lines so they don't get electrocuted. But we shrink from restrictions that are going to save their souls and protect their hearts!

We Have a Mandate from God to Protect Our Children

Sometimes protecting our children means influencing the peers they hang around with. If my child is spending a lot of time with someone who does not have the right attitude or heart toward God, I will speak with my child about the influence that person is having on him and restrict his contact with that person. You might think that is harsh, but I have a mandate from God to protect the spirit of my children, just as much as I have a mandate and responsibility to protect them physically.

Some parents shrink back from this, fearing their child will hate them. I have a baby, and when I restrict him physically for his own safety, he protests. He doesn't like it one bit, but he doesn't hate me. I don't expect him to like it or to understand, I just expect him to obey. In just the same way, I don't expect my teenagers to like everything I do to protect their souls and their spirits, but I still expect them to obey. They don't hate me. Sometimes they may think they do, but I know they don't. I try not to take it personally. After all, I'm the adult, and I'm the one with a mandate from God. I'm not trying to please them; I'm trying to please Him—that makes it a lot easier! Your children won't always like it when you try to hide them from things that can harm them. In fact, sometimes they will hate it. But I can promise you, they won't hate you.

Don't Be Afraid of the World's Edicts

As a parent it takes faith to hide your children. It takes faith to protect them. Listen to what Hebrews 11:23 says,

> *By faith Moses' parents hid him for three months after he was born, because they saw he was no ordinary child, **and they were not afraid of the king's edict.*** (NIV)

Even though the king's edict declared, "Throw the baby in the river!" and even though thousands obeyed that edict out of fear, Moses' mother chose to obey the mandate from God rather than the king's edict. We need to do the same. Don't be afraid of the world's edicts. Parents often hear their children plead: "But everyone else's parents are letting them go to that party!" and "Everyone else lets their kids stay out later than that!" I'm often heard saying, "I don't care if every other mother in the whole world lets her child go to that party, you are not going." It's simple, really: they are not every other child, and I am not every other mother!

It takes faith to rear a child who is not ordinary. And believe me, God never ever intended your child to be "ordinary." Your child has a destiny. God has a plan for his or her life just as surely as He did for Moses' life. Your child may not lead a nation, but he or she still has a vital role to play in God's kingdom.

Train Your Children

The third thing that we learn from Moses' story is to train our children. Proverbs 22:6 says, *"Train up a child in the way he should go, And when he is old he will not depart from it."* That doesn't mean we should train them in the way that *we want them to go* or even train them in the way that *we think that they should go.* It means God has placed a blueprint

> Don't be afraid of the world's edicts dictating what is cool and acceptable for your children.

for greatness within each and every child and, as parents, it is our responsibility and mandate to train them in such a way that steers them in the direction of that blueprint.

The very word used here for *train* means "to initiate" or "to discipline through narrowing." When you train a horse or a dog, you don't let it run wild. Instead, you restrict its movements so that it will develop control and will be attentive to your voice. You narrow the kinds of activities it engages in. A racehorse, for example, is not allowed to run free in the wilderness. It is kept in a more confined and refined environment. All its activities are geared to ensure it can run to its potential. A guide dog is trained from its youth. Its environment is narrowed so that it learns to do what is needed to help blind people. Each is trained with a clear goal in mind.

Keep Your Eyes Fixed on the End Result

So many times I see parents who are making it up as they go along. I've been guilty of this many times myself. It's far easier to be a responder than it is to be a trainer. Being a trainer means having an end goal in mind. It means understanding what you are trying to achieve and keeping your eyes fixed firmly on the end result. To be a trainer, you need to have some idea what your desired result will look like. If I was to ask you, "What kind of adult will your child be?" would you look at me incredulously like some do and say, "How would I know? A good one, I hope!"

> God has placed a blueprint for greatness within each and every child, and it is our responsibility to steer them in that direction.

You see, I know as I write this there are some people in my circle of peers who think I am a little too worried about things, a little overly strict perhaps, a little paranoid or weird. That doesn't worry me unduly because I have caught sight of the end result—not totally, of course, but enough to set my course! So when I ask my son to be home at a certain time, I don't care what time the other kids his age have to go home or what everyone else's mom is saying, because I know he wasn't born to be "any other kid." I have had a glimpse of the plan and I know that I have a big part to play in it. My part is to train him, to narrow the field from "all the things he could do" to those things that will build into him the character he needs to do what God has called him to do.

When I see my two-year-old sink to the floor because he can't get his own way, I could think to myself, "At least he isn't screaming like Mark did and he isn't whining in protest like Nathan." I could walk away and ignore it, but when he's on the floor I see an adult who is uncooperative and who stubbornly refuses to move unless he is given his own way. That's not in the plan, so I go back to him and ask him to get up. I don't allow him to get away with that behavior because I'm training him with a purpose and goal in mind. You see, to be a trainer you need to be consistent.

Remember Proverbs 22:6: we are to train up a child in the way he or she should go, so when he or she is old he or she will not depart from it. A lot of the training we will do with our children will be general: we'll teach them to love God, encourage them to invite Jesus into their lives, train them in obedience, honesty, kindness, and all the other things that are necessary for them to grow into wonderful people. But, supplementary to this, I believe we can start to train them more specifically.

If your child isn't kind by nature, teach him or her to be kind. Make it a focus in your training. Some children are not honest by nature; they are more deceptive. Teach them the value of honesty. If they have a tendency to be lazy, then train them to work hard. You can balance your children's weaknesses so that they do not have to battle alone with them when they are older.

Teach Your Child to Use His or Her Spiritual Gifts

Then there is the training that is even more specific. It is training that is linked to the gifts God gives people at salvation. Each one of us receives spiritual gifts when we give our lives to Christ. Children are no exception. Their gifts will be in immature form, but that should not stop you from teaching them how to use their spiritual gifts. Many of us have seen what God can do with adults who surrender their gifts back to God for Him to use. Imagine what God could do with a child who has been taught how to use his or her gift from a young age. Imagine a child who begins to understand why God put him or her on this planet. Imagine a child who realizes that life is not just about him or her, but about what he or she can do for others!

My oldest son has the gift of discerning spirits. The first time I became aware of this was when we were eating at a Sizzler restaurant and a young waiter came to take our order. We found out later it was his first night and he appeared a bit nervous. Mark was only about five at the time, and after the waiter had left, he leaned over to me and said in a lowered voice, "Mom, he isn't very confident, is he? He's a nice man, though." In fourth grade, Mark's teacher came to school one day after losing her grandmother. She later told me she thought she was hiding her grief well until Mark stood next to her and said, "Miss Bates, are you okay? Do you need a hug?" She burst into tears and had to leave for the day!

> Proverbs 22:6 says, "Train up a child in the way he should go, And when he is old he will not depart from it."

As Mark grew older, I had to help him understand the things he was feeling. Sometimes he gets very agitated with individuals and makes comments like, "I hate that person! He is an idiot!" These were not his peers or people who upset him. These were people who had come into his focus that day, often in a casual encounter. After one of his agitated comments, I said to him, "Just back up a minute, Mark, and see if you can tell me why you just said what you did about that person!" He thought for a moment and responded, "Okay, they are a victim, and they act like the world owes them something. They have a huge chip on their shoulder and don't take responsibility for anything. They also have a problem with authority." I smiled and said to him, "That is a very accurate assessment of that person, but understand that if you say, 'I hate that person, he is an idiot!' you are always going to be corrected, because that is the wrong way to express what you are feeling."

Nathan has a pastoral/coaching gift: he wants to see others be the best that they can be. I first picked it up when he walked off the basketball court one day in utter frustration because his team was not working together even though the coach kept telling them they were doing great. "We aren't doing great, Mom!" he said through frustrated tears. "We are all over the place and no one is listening to me!" He begged me to ask the coach if he could address the team and show them where they should be standing and what they should be doing. He is an encourager, and he loves to show others how to do things. He looks out for those who are discouraged and will give them whatever he thinks they need to feel better. Once it was a pair of Nike shoes!

> Imagine what God could do with a child who has been taught how to use his or her gift from a young age.

Every so often, when Nathan is being unkind, I remind him that part of God's plan for him is to be an encourager and to build people up. He knows it in his own heart, but when I remind him, he smiles and begins to put it into practice. You see, the gift God has given your child will be the area the enemy will try to negate. Nathan has felt the pressure at times to team up with other kids who are being cruel or who end up ostracizing others in the class, but because he knows some of "why God has put me here," he understands when I say to him, "I think the devil is trying to limit your usefulness to God." I have never tried to tell my children what lies within them, but together, with God, we discover it, acknowledge it, and build upon it.

> The gift God has given your child will be the area the enemy will try to negate.

Create God Moments

Develop in Your Children a Hunger for God

Chapter Six

Create God Moments

Develop in Your Children a Hunger for God

*"For He satisfies the thirsty and fills
the hungry with good things."
—Psalm 107:9 (NIV)*

J*ack* is doing drugs!"

These are words every parent dreads to hear. On this occasion, the words came from one of my sons, who had just discovered that one of his peers had strayed off the path he had started on and lost his way. We talked about it for a while, and we discussed the reasons behind such behavior and the types of distractions that can cause kids to turn completely from what they have been taught and embrace the extreme opposite. I asked my son what would stop him from making the same decisions "Jack" had made. He looked at me and said, "Well, firstly, if the drugs didn't kill me, you and Dad would! But also, I just couldn't walk away from God like that."

The sad thing was that this boy didn't just "walk away from God like that." He didn't get up one morning and say, "Okay, I've had enough. I'm changing direction!" Most children, like this boy, change direction ever so slowly. They rarely make sharp right-hand turns. The majority of kids who stray from what they have been taught start straying long before they end up with a joint of marijuana in their mouths. It starts with a heart attitude. That attitude often develops because they are hurting inside, and have built up anger and frustration that have not been addressed. As a mother, one of the best actions you can take is to teach your kids to deal with offense. Make sure that after each altercation you have with them, the air is cleared and their hearts are free from offense. That may mean that you need to go and apologize to them for the way you spoke or for disciplining the wrong person. One of the quickest ways to build up offense in the heart of your child is to be unprepared to say sorry to them when you are wrong.

> There is a fine line between allowing a child a free voice to talk back to you and allowing him to express to you when he is hurt and upset.

As I write this, I know I need to go and talk over an incident with one of my sons. We have both made up, we have both said sorry (yes, I was at fault too), but I'm not convinced that his heart is clear of offense. So I think I need to have a further conversation with him about it.

The Progress toward Rejection

There is a fine line between allowing a child a free voice to talk back to you and allowing him to express to you when he is hurt and upset. If your children feel you have been too busy for them, that you have rejected them in some way, or that you haven't listened to them explain something that was important to them, they are not likely to tell you, as there may be little or no opportunity to do so. These hurts build up over time, and then turn into deep anger that leads to resentment and bitterness. Resentment and bitterness manifest themselves in behavior that rejects anything aligned with the person with whom they are offended...including their belief system.

Before long a child begins to reject what his parents say and do, seeks the company of others who share his hurt, and soon he turns from God. Now, he does this not because he wants to or because he intended to. It's just that God is part of the package that "belongs" to Mom and Dad. Obviously I have just given you many years compacted down into one para-graph, but I believe that is the progression toward a rejection of parents' values and of God, a rejection that leaves parents asking, "What did we do wrong?"

Training Your Children Is a God-Given Responsibility

Sometimes parents do not understand that training is a responsibility entrusted to them by God. As parents, we were dramatically rescued by God from a life of mess and full of sin. We were like the Israelites living in slavery in Egypt until God set us free. We are now living a radically different lifestyle in the Promised Land. What many people don't realize is that God commanded those whom He rescued to then teach and train their children, the children who were born into a new environment, so that they were able to live in the same land in freedom. Many Christian parents are first-generation

Christians: as children, they were never trained in the ways of God, so it doesn't come naturally to them to train their own children. In many cases, their children have never had a "before Christ" and "after Christ" experience, so their children need to be taught in a way different from the way their parents were trained. God's instructions to the children of Israel when they had settled into the Promised Land are equally as applicable to first generation Christian parents. Here is my paraphrase of Deuteronomy 11:1–22, a passage every parent should read over and over again:

> Now train the next generation to love and obey Me so that they will not have to be rescued, but that they might live in the land that I have given to you and to them and their children after them.

Now here is the same Scripture (emphasis added) in the *New Living Translation:*

> *You must love the* Lord *your God and obey all his requirements, laws, regulations, and commands.* **Listen! I am not talking now to your children, who have never experienced the discipline of the** Lord **your God or seen his greatness and awesome power.** *They weren't there to see the miraculous signs and wonders he performed in Egypt against Pharaoh and all his land. They didn't see what the* Lord *did to the armies of Egypt and to their horses and chariots—how he drowned them in the Red Sea as they were chasing you, and how he has kept them devastated to this very day! They didn't see how the* Lord *cared for you in the wilderness until you arrived here. They weren't there to see what he did to Dathan and Abiram (the sons of Eliab, a descendant of Reuben) when the earth opened up and swallowed them, along with their households and tents and every*

*living thing that belonged to them. **But you have seen all the* Lord's *mighty deeds with your own eyes!** There-fore, be careful to obey every command I am giving you today, so you may have strength to go in and occupy the land you are about to enter. If you obey, you will enjoy a long life in the land the* Lord *swore to give to your ancestors and to you, their descendants—a land flowing with milk and honey! For the land you are about to enter and occupy is not like the land of Egypt from which you came, where you planted your seed and dug out irrigation ditches with your foot as in a vegetable garden. It is a land of hills and valleys with plenty of rain—a land that the* Lord *your God cares for. He watches over it day after day throughout the year! If you carefully obey all the commands I am giving you today, and if you love the* Lord *your God with all your heart and soul, and if you worship him, then he will send the rains in their proper seasons so you can harvest crops of grain, grapes for wine, and olives for oil. He will give you lush pastureland for your cattle to graze in, and you yourselves will have plenty to eat....So commit yourselves completely to these words of mine. Tie them to your hands as a reminder, and wear them on your forehead. **Teach them to your children. Talk about them when you are at home and when you are away on a journey, when you are lying down and when you are getting up again. Write them on the doorposts of your house and on your gates, so that as long as the sky remains above the earth, you and your children may flourish in the land the* Lord *swore to give your ancestors.***

Here God was talking to the parents, telling them to now teach their children to follow His Word and instructions. The results would be that they and their children would flourish, that they would live magnificent lives dedicated to serving God as long as they lived, and that they would teach their children who would teach their own children, and the blessings of God would be upon a multi-generational church!

Develop in Your Children a Hunger for God

God said to the parents, "Your children didn't see all the wonderful miracles I did. They didn't experience My power when I brought you out of Egypt. That's why you need to teach them." But I believe God's intention was to go one step further: we are to teach them so that they too can have awesome personal experiences with God for themselves, so that when they teach their children, they are relating their own experience and planting a hunger in them to get to know this God too!

> Train the next generation to love and obey God so that they will not have to be rescued.

I firmly believe that if our children do not have "God moments" scattered liberally throughout their lives, starting at a young age, the only thing that they will have to hang on to during turbulent times (and every child has them!) will be theory rather than experience. Some parents feel their children are too young to understand the things of God, and they dismiss the God experiences that they could be building on.

I remember vividly the day I gave my life to Jesus. I was barely four years of age. The man who was preaching told me that Jesus wanted to be my friend, and I knew that I really wanted to meet Him. So I hopped out of my seat and walked down to the front of the service. They took me to a side room where a lady with massive hair (it was the 60s!) talked with me about God. I can't remember a thing she said; I was looking for Jesus. Then my eyes spotted a picture on the wall of a man with the kindest eyes I had ever seen. I just knew this was Jesus and knew that I loved Him. The woman probably thought I had no idea what I was doing, but she was wrong. That wasn't the end of my experience with Jesus. There would be many times in my life when I would respond to altar calls or have "God moments" in my bedroom where my love for Jesus was refocused and sometimes reconnected.

> Look for "God moments" when your children have the opportunity to experience God in a personal and real way.

Look for "God Moments" For Our Children

As parents, that's what we should be aiming for with our children: looking for "God moments" when our children have the opportunity to experience God in a personal and real way. Many of those experiences for me were at youth camps. That's why I make sure my children are at every camp they could possibly attend—not because I think Jesus can only show up at camps, but because camps put my kids in a God-focused environment where they are more likely to get touched by God than if they weren't there.

One of my sons had a "God moment" at an Assemblies of God state conference we were attending. The boys were with us in the meeting when the speaker challenged us about our heart for souls. He appealed to people to respond if they wanted God to "break their heart" for souls. Ashley and I were sitting in the first few rows (a great place to sit if you want your kids to be impacted by the presence of God!). We stood and left the boys in their seats as we knelt at the front. The Spirit of God began moving and most of us were weeping. As I shifted my position, out of the corner of my eye I spotted my eldest son, who was about nine at the time, kneeling close by, weeping and rocking in grief as God broke his little heart for those who were lost to God. Moments like these stay with our children for a lifetime. These are times when they feel God, times when they hear God, sticky moments in which they are bonded a little closer to God. These moments produce glue that helps them "stick" when others around them are "peeling off."

I had been asked to speak at a South Australian children's rally on a Saturday. I found myself wishing I could skip Saturday and wake up on Sunday morning after it was all over. Kids are scary to talk to; they aren't going to pretend they are interested in what you have to say. You either have their attention or you don't, and when you don't, you might as well stop speaking and sit down straight away; it's far less painful. I had tried to prepare, but went to bed with a blank mind (quite a common occurrence for me, I might add). As I was preparing to drift off to sleep, a flood of thoughts entered my mind, and because I was sort of expecting God to give me something (I had threatened not to show up unless He did!), I quickly began to jot the thoughts down on the paper I had beside my bed. The ideas involved someone else acting for me on stage, and I thought my son, Nathan, would jump at the chance. He was turning twelve in a week and lately, however, with all those hormones, he was becoming a lot less predictable!

In the morning I asked him if he would help me act out my message. I even threw in a twenty-dollar bribe, but it was all to no avail. He was adamant he didn't want to do it. Rather than resorting to manipulation (that is, any more manipulation)—something that mothers can be very good at with their children—I decided I would appeal to a higher power. I sent up a prayer and said, "God, You know how I need Nathan to help me with *Your* idea? Well, *You* need to convince him to do it." I had twenty-four hours before I had to speak. That was plenty of time for God to work on him. Saturday morning dawned and I had lost hope of Nathan being my helper. So I called the children's pastor to ask him to find me a "volunteer" to help me out. When I hung up the phone, Nathan walked out of his room and declared, "Mom, I'll do it." (Don't you love their timing?!) "Are you sure?" I asked him. He was sure!

I silently thanked God, and we drove to the rally and had a great time. I taught the kids that God had a special journey planned for each one of them and that they received the ticket for their journey when they asked Jesus into their hearts. Some kids thought they should wait until they were older to start that journey. But I told them God intended for them to start right away. He had given them a road map, the Bible, as well as a guide, the Holy Spirit, and a suitcase with some special things inside. I told them God had put in each person's suitcase special gifts he or she could take along on the journey and that they would be able to give away these gifts to others to help them on their journey.

Nathan opened the suitcase we had brought with us. In it was a bag marked "Encouragement," and inside that bag were cards with encouraging words written on them, as well as a bunch of inspirational stickers that he gave away to kids in the crowd. (I was so touched when he gave the first card to a young boy in a wheelchair!) The next bag he took out was a huge bag marked "Giving," filled with candy. Together we caused a riot as four hundred kids stormed the stage when we started throwing candy around. We eventually managed to restore order and keep the meeting on track.

"Mom, I Know What the Holy Spirit Sounds Like"

When Nathan had finished and was about to sit down, I called him back and said to him, "Nathan, this is for you." I picked up another bag not in the suitcase that was marked "Joy," and said, "Because you have been unselfish and given those gifts away, now God has a gift for you." I handed him an enormous bag of his very own candy! You should have seen his eyes! The next evening, sitting in church while the preacher gave the altar call, Nathan sidled up to me and said in a loud whisper, "Mom, I know what the Holy Spirit sounds like." He had my attention! It's not the kind of comment you expect from a twelve-year-old male!

"Do you?" I asked. "What does He sound like?"

"Well, you don't hear Him up here," he said, pointing to his head. "You hear him down here," and he pointed to his heart.

I nodded, but he wasn't finished yet.

"I Wanted to Give That Money to God"

"And you don't really hear Him as much as you feel Him," he went on. "Mom, you know the other day when you asked me to help you and I said no? Well, all day after that I felt like a hand pushing me on the inside and a voice saying to me, 'You need to do it, Nathan! You need to do it, Nathan!' It was like a nagging voice and a pushing hand." I found out later that he had put the twenty dollars I had given him the day before into the offering bag that morning in church. He explained to me later, "I got a huge bag of candy, and also God has already rewarded me with a bag of 'Joy.' I felt so good after helping you, Mom, that I wanted to give that money to God." This was a moment—a moment in time when you as a parent realize your child has just had a revelation that will be part of his experience of God forever, a foundation-laying moment that God will continue to build on.

> "Commit yourselves wholeheartedly to these commands I am giving you today. Repeat them again and again to your children."

It's the kind of thing I believe Moses was talking about in Deuteronomy 6:4–9 (NLT) when he said,

> *Hear, O Israel! The LORD is our God, the LORD alone. And you must love the LORD your God with all your heart, all your soul, and all your strength. And you must commit yourselves wholeheartedly to these commands I am giving you today. Repeat them again and again to your children. Talk about them when you are at home and when you are away on a journey, when you are lying down and when you are getting up again. Tie them to your hands as a reminder, and wear them on your forehead. Write them on the doorposts of your house and on your gates.*

Life presents us with so many opportunities to share God's principles with our children. My prayer as a mother is that I don't miss too many of them! It's so easy to get distracted, to feel too weary to engage in yet another argument, that you almost miss the opportunity right in front of you. I'm sure I missed many such opportunities, but I sure remember the ones I didn't!

My sons' school had a rule that only white sneakers were to be worn for sports. Now, that seems like a fairly reasonable rule until you talk to your nine-year-old and realize that only black sneakers are cool. The day before sports day we had a discussion in our house about the "stupidity" of certain school rules, and the fact that "every other child in the whole school is allowed to wear black sneakers." (That was because their parents understood that when the school said "white sneakers" it didn't really mean "white sneakers.") Even more pressing was the argument that "I can't run very fast in my white sneakers. They make my feet sore!"

What do you do when you hear yourself saying, "You have to wear them because that is the rule!" and at the same time you are thinking, "Why can't I think of something more intelligent to say? I sound just like my mom!" (Not that my mom wasn't intelligent; in fact, quite the opposite, but I always hated answers that didn't have a good reason attached to them.) I ended the already-too-lengthy discussion by saying I would talk about it in the morning, and escaped from Mark's room feeling a little defeated.

I attacked the ironing as I pondered my insufficient ability to think up really good answers for a nine-year-old expert in rationality. Ironing is always a great time for me. It's when I'm still and quiet long enough for God to interrupt me. I must have only been on to the second shirt when, out of the blue, the familiar still, small voice said, "Go back into his room and ask him if he thinks it would be okay to break one of God's rules if the end result was guaranteed to be positive." I finished the shirt and checked to see if my nine-year-old was still awake. (Why I did this I don't know, because if God told me to go back to his room, then he had to still be awake!) I sat on his bed and said, "Mark, can I ask you a question?"

"Sure, Mom." (He considered himself a bit of an expert on questions, but then I'm told most nine-year-olds do!)

"Would it be okay to break one of God's rules if the end results were guaranteed to be good?" I asked.

There was a pause as he digested the question. Then came the categorical reply: "No!"

"Why not?" I asked, smelling victory in the air! "What if someone was saved as a result of you breaking God's rule? Would it be okay then?"

"No, Mom!" he said, shifting a little too easily into the role of teacher! "It would be good if the person got saved. God would like that. But it's the person who broke the rule who would have to take the consequences. Things might be okay in the short term, but it's the long term you have to think about."

He Would Never Be a Loser if He Kept God's Rules

What happened next was one of those golden moments in parenting, when you know you have the right thing to say and you don't even have to bluff! I looked at him square in the eye and said, "Son, God wants you to wear your white sneakers in the morning because He wants you to learn that it's not worth breaking a rule just to get a good result in the short term." He looked at me with a grin (a loser's grin!) and said,

"Okay, Mom." He might have thought he'd lost the argument, but I knew right then that this was the making of a champion. He would never be a loser if he kept God's rules. I told him so too. I told him God would bless him for obeying the rules that had been made by those in authority over him.

Sports day was a scorcher, and the usual mayhem reigned as we scattered around the house filling drink bottles and applying sunscreen. The black sneakers were forgotten (or at least abandoned) for the white ones, and we were focused on the day ahead. Now, Mark is a talented sportsman, particularly when it comes to bat-and-ball sports. Unfortunately, they aren't included in the average school sports day. When it comes to running, he is by no means a tortoise, but he had never made it to a finals race.

Ashley and I lined up with the other parents at the finish line to cheer our children home, camera in hand to capture the moment. The whistle blew (a nice change from the starter's gun of previous years that would have some of the kids still standing shell-shocked at the starting line while others were finishing the race!) and they were off. I watched as my son ran in his white sneakers that weren't trendy and "hurt his feet" as he pounded the turf. I know some of the other parents would have thought I was overly sentimental when I cried, because he won second place in his heat...and a place in the final! But he knew what I meant when I gave him a hug and said, "It must have been the sneakers." He didn't win in the final race, nor did he get a placing. In fact, he came in last. But as far as we were concerned, he was way out in front.

Children Learn a Lot from Watching Us

I somehow think God knows that we learn more if the lessons are real-life situations and the outcomes are measurable. He also knows that children learn a whole lot more from *watching* us than they do from listening to what we *say*. Those verses in Deuteronomy 6 aren't just saying, "Sit your kids down and have devotions with them." In fact, if they were, my lack of consistency would mean I have failed miserably.

Devotions are a great start, but I believe Moses was actually saying, "Teach them God's Word and His commandments (that's the 'when you are at home' part), but then you also need to apply them when you are outside the home." In other words, you actually are supposed to live what you teach. When you are lost and you can't find your way,

> Children learn a whole lot more from watching us than they do from listening to what we say.

stop to pray and ask God to help you. Teach your children the power of prayer in everyday situations...even *you* may be surprised, as I have many times, at the way God answers when you call!

When you are driving your car in a hurry and someone pulls out in front of you, remember that your kids are watching. That's when you can teach them to "love your neighbor as yourself"! Seriously, as the boys have grown older, I have used those frustrating situations to teach them the road rules. "See that man?" I would ask. "He's stuck out in the middle of the road to turn right. When you boys drive, remember to get over to the right and remember that you are not the only person on the road." Well, it helps me anyway; it takes the pressure off trying to respond with a gracious smile. I can address his foolishness while teaching my children to avoid it! One of the biggest spiritual turn-offs is the unfortunate tendency for many parents to live one way at home and another in public or at church. Kids are astute. At a very young age they are able to pick up on the fact that what you say or tell them to do is not really what you live.

Don't Make Devotions a Struggle or an Event

Don't make devotions a struggle or an event that your children dread or the activity you subject them to at the dinner table. Make devotions a thing you do when you are walking with them, driving them in the car, or taking them to tennis lessons. Listen for the opportunities, the comments they make that say, "Hey, I've been thinking about this."

> Make devotions a thing you do when you are walking with them or driving with them in the car. Listen for the opportunities.

I remember walking down a street in Queensland with one of my boys not that long ago. We had walked in comfortable silence for about five minutes when he said, "I don't have a choice, do I?" Now, we had not been talking about anything to do with choices or any other relevant subject, but somehow I knew he was talking about the call of God on his life. I quietly replied, "Of course you do; we all have a choice."

He scoffed a little and said, "Some choice! If I walk away I'll be miserable for the rest of my life!"

"It will still be your choice," I said.

Then the opportunity was gone, the conversation was over, and we walked on again in silence.

Set Fixed Principles in Your Family Life

Yes, I pray for my children often, but I also make sure I place them in positions where they are likely to encounter God. For instance, we have a fixed position in our home: on Sundays we attend God's house at least twice. This is a fixed position. It's set in concrete. No one tries to alter that position because it has been "set in place" in our home. I don't have my kids asking me, "Mom, can I go to this party on Sunday night?" They don't even ask, because it is fixed in position.

If you are building a secure structure, there are some essential components that you have to fix into place first. For instance, when building a house, the foundation needs to be set first, then columns and beams have to be fixed into place. These ensure the structure is strong and will not fall under pressure. We have built some structures and supports into our family life that are fixed; they are central principles that do not move. They simply never move. One of these is to meet together with other believers, to make God's house a place where we love to go. Hebrews 10:25 encourages us not to move away from this fixed position of meeting together.

Why have we chosen this fixed position for our household? Because we know that God's house is the best place in which to be. It is the place where we receive encouragement for daily living, the place where our faith is boosted, the place where we are taught the principles that are going to make us successful in life, and the place where we and our kids can encounter God and have life-changing experiences that will shape our future.

If this isn't tied down in our lives, if it isn't a fixed position, then when the foundations shake it will move. When we face difficult circumstances (and we all do!), we will shrink back into our own little world and our focus turns to ourselves rather than to others. Before long it affects our fellowship with one another. You see, it's easier to stay away than to face those who have hurt us. It's easier to sleep in on Sunday mornings than to make the effort to get up and go to church. It's easier to finish reading the newspaper on Sunday than to push ourselves to finish everything on Saturday so we can be in church on Sunday. It then becomes too easy for our children to also feel like sleeping in on Sunday when we want them to be in church.

> Place your children into positions where they are more likely to encounter God, such as church or youth camps.

Sometimes it takes a sacrifice on my part to keep placing my kids in environments where they can encounter God. Often there are financial sacrifices to this! It costs money to go to all those youth camps and conferences, and it's even more expensive if you take your kids to the events you have to go to as well! Sometimes it's a lot easier to leave your kids home. It's a lot easier if you don't have to discipline them to sit in meetings without causing a major disruption. Believe me, we've done our fair share of those! (A loud belch at the wrong moment can crush any dignity you thought you might have had!)

When Mark was born I remember many well-meaning people saying to me, "When I was your age, I just concentrated on the children. It was a season in my life, and you need to do the same." While they were completely correct, my focus needed to be the family that God had given me, including our church family. I had a strange stirring in my spirit that it had to be possible to focus on both: to serve God in the way He had called me, to make sure my children were not just given the attention that a nanny could give them, and also to nourish them emotionally and spiritually. And yet I had so much advice to the contrary that it upset me deeply. I got down on my knees before God and began to ask Him for some direction. I remember opening my Bible and, through the tears, reading: "Take Mark and bring him with you for he is profitable to Me for the ministry" (2 Timothy 4:11). It is marked November 1988 in the margin of my Bible. Not only did it answer my dilemma, but it was the first glimpse I had of the blueprint for his life, when he was just one month old.

Since that time I have been determined to take my children everywhere I go. I promise you, though, that it has not always been easy. For a start, both the older boys were extremely active when they were younger. (Who am I kidding? They are still very active!) But because I have settled what I am supposed to be doing, it is easier for me to help them adjust to what God wants them to do.

God called me; He planned my life and then gave me three wonderful boys who all have within their DNA the capability of adapting to the life to which Ashley and I are called. Many times I have looked in envy at other children sleeping peacefully under pews in church and wondered why all three of mine somehow missed out on that gene! Then again, when the meeting is over and my children are still playing happily (okay, running wild!) and the children who were sleeping are now awake and grumbling, begging to be taken home, I begin to understand God's wisdom because we are always the last to leave!

Our Children Absorb Our Attitude toward Church

Many times I am asked, "How did you and Ashley manage taking the kids everywhere with you?" or "How did the kids cope?" or "Don't they feel resentful at being dragged everywhere?" First, I have found that my children will absorb the attitude I have toward my work and toward God's house. If I am feeling flat and don't feel like getting up for church on Sunday morning, it will be even harder to get the children excited about going. But if I am excited about God's house, then they will be too.

Last weekend Ashley and I were on vacation following a huge year. We had intended to visit another church in the city, but had woken up too late to get there on time. We staggered out of the bedroom to be greeted by our kids with, "What are you doing? Hurry up, you guys! Do you know what the time is? You're going to be late for church!" We grinned, realizing that the tables had been turned, and our two teenagers were chiding us for being tardy!

> I have found that my children will absorb the attitude I have toward my work and toward God's house.

Second, Ashley and I have committed to making church fun for our boys. We are often the last ones to leave the church building after each service, so we have allowed the boys to go to Ashley's office while they are waiting for us. More recently we have allowed them to get something to eat from the café and put it on our tab. I have learned that to make them sit still and wait for us is inviting an argument in the front row; bored, hungry boys are not easily restrained! I don't want their memories of church to be clouded by long waits while Mom and Dad finish talking to people. We also have made it a tradition on Sunday nights after church to go home via the local McDonald's drive-through. We arrive home and sit down together to chat about the day or to watch something on television.

When the boys were younger and we took them to a lot of conferences, I would buy them a small present for each day of the conference. I would wrap up the gifts and give them to the boys at the beginning of each meeting. I would tell them they couldn't open their present until the singing was over and I expected them to stand and join in the singing. I've never seen kids so eager for the preaching to start! They would then play with that toy and other toys I would bring in their "conference pack." This pack might include some new snacks they hadn't tried before, a drink, a puzzle book, and so on. It may have cost me about fifty dollars per conference, but it was worth every cent. It became something they actually looked forward to. Now, it did get harder as they grew older; the toys became a lot more expensive. But by then, the boys were old enough to understand the principle of give and take. We would take them to a conference and the deal was that they had to sit for three days of meetings in order to get three days of skiing at the end of the conference. (Don't do the skiing at the beginning; you have a lot less bargaining power!)

Ashley and I remember a moment when we were sitting around our kitchen table discussing where we would go for our next vacation. The boys were quite young, and one of them, bursting with excitement, asked, "Can we go to that place with the ducks?" Responding to our blank looks, he said, "You know, the one with all the animals and it had a lake with boats on it? Please, please can we go back there?" His brother chimed in with enthusiastic agreement as Ashley and I racked our brains trying to remember the location. Eventually it dawned on us: they were talking about a conference venue we had been to about a year earlier. They had spent a week at a place called Hochsteins in the Adelaide Hills. The conference schedule had been jam-packed, but at the end of the week before we went home, Ashley and I rented two canoes and rowed the boys out on the tiny lake. We played with them on the playground equipment and wandered over to the animal enclosure to see the emus. Ashley and I looked at each other in amazement. All we remembered was a week-long conference and all the boys remembered was the hour or so we spent with them at the end of the week. Memories like that are so easy to make—don't miss the opportunities.

Every Mother Knows You Are What You Eat!

"What's for dinner tonight, Mom?" I cringe every time I hear that question because I know someone is not going to be happy with the choice I have made. I try my best to provide nutritious meals that are tasty, well-balanced, and appealing to the taste buds of three men and a baby, but I rarely get it right! On the occasional night when I hear, "Oh, thanks, Mom! You're a legend!" it's usually because I have placed a pizza in front of them! Now, I have to say that despite the years of adversity I have suffered in this area, I refuse to let my kitchen become a restaurant in which each family member can order his own meal the *way* he likes it and *when* he likes it. In fact, my boys will tell you that one of the sayings they will remember me for is, "This is not a restaurant!"

The rules are simple: I serve dinner and they eat it, whether they like it or not! Well, I do make exceptions for personal taste: Ashley doesn't like pumpkin, Mark doesn't like mushrooms, and Nathan hates peas, pumpkin, mushrooms, squash, zucchini, cauliflower, any kind of casserole that looks different, any kind of spicy or curried dish, potatoes that haven't been made into fries...I'm sure you get the picture! As for me, I love my food (even Brussels sprouts!). There are very few foods I won't eat, so it has been a huge shock to have a child who only likes pizza and fries and will eat very little else without making World War III out of the meal. Nathan is nearly fourteen and, for all you mothers in the same situation, I am afraid to admit there has been very little improvement over the years. My goal now is trying to deliver him as healthy as I can to his future bride, and grin every inch of her slow walk up the aisle, knowing that the poor girl will have her work cut out for her feeding him!

> Everything we say and do, every attitude and response, is being absorbed by our children, whether it is negative talk or praise.

As mothers, we serve up a lot more than just meals. Everything we say and do, every attitude and response, is being hungrily consumed by our children, whether we like it or not. Whatever you set before your children, they will consume, whether it is negative talk, criticism, praise, or a poverty mentality. I can promise you they will eat what you serve, and every mother knows that you are what you eat!

Lessons in Faith

Teach Them to Believe God for Themselves

Lessons in Faith

Teach Them to Believe God for Themselves

"Now faith is being sure of what we hope for and certain of what we do not see."
—Hebrews 11:1 (NIV)

"M om, can we get a basketball hoop? Dad promised we could get one!"

It was one of the hardest times in my life. My husband was in the middle of a burnout, we were building a house that now had become my responsibility to manage, and like many couples who build, we had absolutely no money to spare. In fact, we didn't even have enough money to put concrete down around the house. And now my son was asking me for a basketball hoop! I took a deep breath. The boys didn't know that Ashley was sick. Actually, it would be over ten years before we told them the story. So I knew I needed some inspiration quickly. I was determined to use the situation as a teaching tool, but I felt like the weight of the world was on my shoulders.

I shifted in my seat, and as quickly as I had done that, I shifted the weight of my son's question onto the only shoulders I knew could carry it at the moment: God's. "Honey, we don't have the money right now to buy that basketball hoop, but God does. Maybe we should ask Him for one?" I began to sing a little song I remembered from Sunday school: "He owns the cattle on a thousand hills, the wealth in every mine. He owns the rivers and the rocks and hills, the sun and stars that shine..."

"Let's ask God to sell a cow," I suggested. "That will give us enough money for a basketball hoop." The mood lightened and Nathan said, "What if He sold a diamond, Mom? Then we could afford hundreds of basketball hoops!" I began to think of all the *other* things we could buy, like carpet for the new house and concrete for the paths! That night, when my son went to bed, he prayed for that basketball hoop with the assurance in his heart that it was as easy for God as selling a cow! I silently wished I had his faith.

At the time, Ashley and I were youth pastors at Paradise Community Church in Adelaide, and our youth camp was only a few days away. I left the boys with my mother-in-law and we went to camp that weekend with only one dollar in the bank to keep the account open. No one knew about our situation. I hadn't told a soul, and besides, I had a lot more to worry about than just finances. The camp was fantastic. Before the final meeting, I felt a strong impulse to drive home (we were in the Adelaide Hills at a place called Hochsteins) to pick up the boys. They were sitting in the front row with us during that last meeting. The speaker stood at the beginning of the meeting and said,

"I've never done this before" (that always makes me nervous!), "but I was sitting in my spa before I got ready for this meeting and God spoke to me and said, 'Ashley and Jane are going on a vacation'" (actually, we were taking six weeks leave without pay as Ashley needed time out to recover) "'and they have no money at all.' So here's what I feel to do: we are going to take up an offering for them to bless them."

Now, you probably think that that would have made me very happy, but I have never felt so helpless or so humbled in my entire life. I also have never felt such an incredible presence of God as in that meeting. I fell to my knees and began to weep. People in the meeting were also crying as they took up an offering that day. After I had composed myself, I took the microphone and told them of the "basketball hoop" conversation I had with the boys in the car that week. I looked at my boys in the front row (they were also teary) and said, "Boys, God just sold a few cows for us today!" In actual fact, it was more like a few diamonds! We were able to go away for a vacation, we had enough money to carpet the house and lay the concrete around the house, and we went out and bought the biggest and best basketball hoop we could find! After that, it wasn't hard for the boys to believe that God could provide for all their needs. They knew Mom and Dad didn't always have the means to provide, but God could, and would, if they asked.

God Provides a PlayStation

On another occasion, Mark asked us for a PlayStation. He was one of the only boys in his class without one (that's what he told us, anyway!) and he had been asking for one for months. There were so many other things that we needed before we could spend money on a PlayStation, so we told him to ask God for one. We prayed about it and I thought nothing more of it. A few days later we were at McDonald's. I'd had one of "those" days and had given in to the pitiful cries of my children, who were complaining about the lack of McDonald's food in their diet. We sat down at a table and the place-mat advertised a competition: design your own McDonald's Christmas card and you could win...a PlayStation! Mark's eyes lit up and he declared, "I'm going to win this!"

He went home with characteristic focus that comes with anything he puts his mind to. He drew a Christmas card, asked for my advice about the colors, and spent the ensuing hours coloring in his card. He mailed it off and, sure enough, a few weeks later we were notified that Mark had won and we were asked to go and collect his prize. When I told him he had won, he announced, "I knew I would! It is God giving me the PlayStation that I asked Him for!"

"I'm Going to America!"

When Mark was in fourth grade, his father went to America. Mark was desperate to go with him, but we said that we couldn't afford for him to go as well. As Ashley left, Mark pointed to him and said, "Next time I'm coming with you!" "You'd better talk to God about that!" Ashley replied. I should have known he would! The next time I looked at his computer, he had placed the American flag and the words "I'm going to America" on his computer screen as "wallpaper," so that every time he turned on his computer that's what he would see. Every night when I would pray with him, he never forgot to ask God about going to America. Six months passed and he was still praying every night for God to provide him with a trip to America.

Some time later, Ashley went on a trip to Melbourne to a crusade at which an American evangelist was the guest speaker. He was invited to breakfast with this evangelist and a number of other people. Several of those who were invited failed to turn up that morning, so at the breakfast table there was Ashley, two other gentlemen, and the evangelist. The two other men were engaged in deep conversation, which left Ashley to talk with the evangelist, whom he had never met before. They exchanged introductions and began to talk to one another. At one point in the conversation the evangelist had a strange look on his face and he said to Ashley, "I'm bringing you to America!" He then paused and added, "In fact, I'm bringing you and your wife and your kids to America too." Ashley was so surprised! This man, who had only just met Ashley an hour ago, was inviting him to America and offering to pay to bring his wife and children over too!

> Some children don't wear their heart on their sleeve. It takes time to connect with their heart.

Ashley came home that day and told me what had happened. All I could think of was that I owed this miracle to the faith of my son who had pestered God every day for six months until God gave him his dream! I drove straight to the school that day. (I know I should have waited until we were sure this man would come good on his promise. I know I should have been more cautious, but faith isn't cautious, it's bold!...and I'm impulsive!) I knocked on Mark's classroom door and called him out of class. I said to him, "Guess what?" His first response was, "We're getting a dog?" (He had been asking us for a dog for ages too!) "No," I said. "Even bigger!" "We are going to America?" "Yes!" I nodded as tears poured down my face. He joined me as we celebrated his faith together and the goodness of a God who responds to faith, no matter whose it is.

> Grudges want you to pick them up and nurse them. But grudges that are fed begin to grow and before long they turn into resentment.

We went to America that August. The evangelist paid for our flights and our accommodation at the Disney World Resort, and he gave us a seven-day "park-hopper pass" to all five Disney parks! What an awesome God we serve! And it's no wonder that when my son broke his arm in two places while skating that he had no problem believing God could heal him. A week later he was swinging off the doorpost to prove to me that he was healed! Now it's my kids who say to me, "Mom, where's your faith?"

God Can Change the Heart of a Schoolboy

Nathan's faith was tested in different ways. When he switched schools in fourth grade, he had no trouble making friends. In fact, he came home on his first day and said, "Mom, one of my new friends is a pastor's kid too, and it's okay to be a pastor's kid at this new school." There was one boy, however, who seemed to control his friendships with all the other boys. This boy was one of the most popular boys in the class. Nathan kept his struggle to himself for six months. I knew he was struggling with something, because he was angry and would take it out on the family when he got home. Whenever I asked him what was wrong, he spoke only of his immediate gripe with whoever was annoying him at the time.

Finally, one night, things came to a head. I had just had to discipline Nathan for yet another angry outburst and I had asked him to go to his room. We began to talk. I was determined not to leave his room until I knew what was eating away at his spirit. (That in itself was risky; I knew it might take hours!) For the first half an hour he just talked through things that had made him angry recently, little incidents around the home. But I knew we had not reached the real issue.

I began to talk to him about the fact that his reaction to each offense did not match the "crime" that had been committed against him and that somewhere deep inside him was a reservoir full of anger. Every time someone did something to annoy him, it was like turning a tap on. I explained to him that instead of a small trickle of anger that was appropriate to the offense, a huge torrent came out that nearly washed us all away. He smiled at this metaphor, as he loves to think in pictures. Then I asked him what it was that made the reservoir so full.

He began to break as he told me about the rejection and the control of this other boy in his class. He told me how he had tried so many times to be nice to him, but it was as if this boy just "slapped his face" in return. He felt so discouraged and saw no way out of the tremendous pressure he felt and the persecution this boy was causing. My heart broke for him. It hadn't been easy for Nathan to change schools. I gently told him I understood how he was feeling and that I thought this boy wasn't really mean; he probably saw Nathan as a threat to his popularity and this was how he was choosing to control that threat. I told him that God cared about the hurt he was feeling and that if we prayed God could change this boy's heart.

117

"No way!" said Nathan. "You don't know this boy, Mom. It's not possible, I've tried everything!"

"Have you prayed?" I asked.

"No, but..."

"Then what have you got to lose? You've tried everything else; it can't hurt to pray. The Bible says even the heart of a king lies in the palm of God's hand and he can turn it whichever way he wants to. If that's the case, surely God can change the heart of a schoolboy?"

"Okay, you pray!" he suggested.

I prayed first, then I asked him to pray as well. When he finished, I tucked him in and he went off to sleep. It had been nearly two hours since we had begun our talk. You see, Nathan doesn't wear his heart on his sleeve like his older brother. It takes time to connect with his heart. You have to peel him like an onion, gently, one layer at a time, until he feels ready to share and safe enough to trust you with his heart. I have to confess, as a busy mom I have failed him so many times. I wish I could say it didn't take me six months to find out what was affecting his spirit, but it did.

The next day he came home from school and called me into his room; he didn't want to talk about it in front of his brother. "Mom, you'll never guess what happened today! I was putting my books on my desk in the classroom and 'John' (not his real name) walked in. I said, 'Hi, John!' He looked up at me, smiled and said, 'Hi, Nathan! Do you want to play basketball with us today?'" Nathan was beaming from ear to ear as he shared this with me. He said to me, "Mom, when we prayed last night I believed God could do it, but I didn't believe for one moment He would do it that quick!" From that day on, Nathan and "John" became good friends and they stayed good friends until John left the school two years later.

Don't Hug a Grudge

I have since learned to take notice of the signs of a full anger reservoir a lot earlier! Nathan is the kind of person who feels things very deeply and tends to hold onto a grudge or a hurt. When he was little, my mother gave me a delightful book that I read to him over and over again called *Don't Hug a Grudge*.[1] The book begins by telling you that grudges can appear very small and harmless, and they are especially fond of people who do not forgive easily. Grudges want you to pick them up and nurse them. But the book warns against doing this because when you do you are feeding them, and grudges that are fed begin to grow and before long they turn into resentment.

Resentment is not as easy to walk away from. You can't hold resentment; it holds you. And if you continue to feed resentment, it turns into bitterness. Bitterness squeezes your mind, makes you do hurtful things to others, and worst of all, draws you away from God.

> If the enemy can damage your child's soft heart through hurt and offense, he has rendered ineffective the very tool God put within your child to help others.

The solution the book gives you is to wash your mind with the water of God's Word and "be kind, tenderhearted, forgiving one another." The message is powerful and the illustrations are endearing. I have used it over and over again. Every so often I threaten to get it out and read it to Nathan again.

He takes time to open up. He needs to be heard and to have his emotions validated. (Hey, don't we all?) Along with his kind heart and sensitive spirit comes a sensitivity to being hurt. The very thing that is his strength is also his biggest area of vulnerability. If the enemy can damage Nathan's soft heart and cause it to become hardened through hurt and offense, then he has rendered ineffective the very tool God put within him to help others.

Keep Their Heart, Because out of It Flow the Issues of Life

Nathan is a natural coach and encourager, just like his father. He loves to help others. Just the other day, as we drove from the city back to our hotel in Malaysia, we passed a slum area of poorly built shanty houses. Nathan turned to me and with compassion in his eyes said, "Mom, don't you just want to buy all those people a house?" That kind of heart needs to be protected from damage so he can allow it to stay soft and pliable in God's hands. Teach children with sensitive hearts (especially boys) that it is a gift to be sensitive, but also that it means they need to "keep their heart, because out of it flow the issues of life."

Keeping their heart means making sure that reservoir inside them is kept drained of anger and hurt. Don't do what I have done and leave it for months before you address the issues of their heart. Teach them to communicate their feelings in a safe environment. Never disregard their feelings as trivial or unimportant.

I remember that when Nathan was a toddler, if I ever gave him a cookie that was broken, even slightly, or if his cookie broke when he was eating it, it was like the end of the world.

It used to really annoy me, especially when we were out and I could do nothing about his silly cookie! Then one day God challenged me to get on my knees at his level and begin to see the world through the eyes of a little boy who wanted his world to be perfect. I saw that day that a broken cookie was a big thing in his world, and that I was disregarding his feelings by telling him there was nothing wrong with his cookie. All of a sudden I could see that there *was* something wrong with his cookie: it was broken. As soon as I began to validate his sorrow at the broken cookie, he would say, "It's okay, Mom!" and he would eat it! All he wanted was for me to acknowledge his distress at the breaking of something that was special to him.

> Teach children with sensitive hearts that it is a gift to be sensitive, but also that it means they need to "keep their heart."

Lessons in faith for Mark look totally different from lessons in faith for Nathan. Nathan always has money, yet money doesn't really mean much to him. He can give it away easily, and he often does. Faith for him is asking God to help him forgive someone who has hurt him. Faith for him is letting go when everything in him wants to get revenge. Faith is trusting God to act on his behalf when things just don't seem fair.

Faith for anyone is believing that we have the things that we can't yet see.

First Teach Them to Face the Little Challenges

Your children will face challenges unique to their own personality and gifting. In order to grow and conquer their areas of weakness, each one of them will need to develop faith to overcome each challenge. They may begin to believe God for a basketball hoop or a PlayStation before they can believe God to go to America. They may have to learn how to deal with broken cookies before they can learn to deal with a broken heart. Teach your children to face the lion and the bear so that when their Goliath turns up they can run at him with the tools God has placed in their hands and slay him without a second thought. The attitudes and principles you teach them when they face the little challenges of life will equip them to deal with the bigger challenges. As they grow, so does the size of their challenges.

Right now, their problem might be the frustration they display when their tower of blocks keeps falling down. If you as a mother can help them tackle these little problems and work through the frustration they feel and the responses they exhibit, then later, when a bigger challenge comes their way, you have already set down the principles and patterns for right responses. Every challenge is really just an opportunity to grow. Think about your own life. God doesn't waste any of the experiences you go through. Even the unpleasant ones God can turn around for our good; we can grow stronger through pain, we can be healed through forgiveness, and we can build our faith and trust in God as we allow Him to be our very present help in times of trouble. Who knows, your kids might just be watching!

---

[1] *Don't Hug a Grudge.* (Story by Donna Perugini, illustrations by Nancy Titolo, published by Little Castle Books, 1987).

Chapter Eight

When You're Not Watching

Let God Be Your Second Pair of Eyes

When You're Not Watching
Let God Be Your Second Pair of Eyes

*"The LORD is watching everywhere, keeping his eye on
both the evil and the good."*
—*Proverbs 15:3 (NLT)*

Mom, Nathan is in the swimming pool!"

My heart lurched! I threw the wallet I was holding in the general direction of my husband and bolted out the door.

We were enjoying a break on Daydream Island in North Queensland, Australia. The boys needed flip-flops because the coral sand was cutting their feet, so I had entered a shop about twenty feet from the deep end of the resort's swimming pool. Nathan was about four at the time, and he had an all-consuming fear of water. When he was younger he had to wear tubes in his ears because he had suffered constant ear infections. When his tubes were in place, he was not allowed to put his head under water. Shower and bath times were a constant struggle; we would both end up exhausted, Nathan from fighting to stay alive and I from trying to reassure him that he would live through the experience!

Nathan had been sitting with Mark on the edge of the pool. Without thinking, I had called Mark away to try on a pair of sandals. (Okay, I know you wouldn't have done that, but I told you I'm not the perfect mother!) When Mark returned to where Nathan had been sitting, he realized Nathan had fallen into the pool!

I raced to the deep end of the pool where he had been sitting and looked over the edge, my heart pounding, sick with fear. As I reached the edge, Nathan's head shot out of the water in front of me and his little hands grasped the edge of the pool firmly. I reached out and pulled his coughing and spluttering form out of the pool, and placed him over my knee. He vomited a large amount of water and began to cry. It was like music to my ears. When he stopped crying I asked him what had happened. He said, "Mommy, I was reading the letters on the side of the pool [the depth indicators] and I fell in. I went right to the bottom. Then Jesus spoke to me and said, 'Nathan, put your feet on the bottom and walk to the side.' I jumped up and you caught me."

I was in tears. So was Ashley, as we realized that God had just intervened, despite our lack of attention. The biggest part of the miracle was that by the time we walked to the other side of the island, Nathan was begging us to go back into the pool. When we returned to the pool, we looked at one another in amazement as he called out to us, "Watch me! I can swim like a fish!" Under the water he went, eyes open and a big smile on his face.

What the Enemy Meant for Bad, God Turned Around for Good

At the end of the vacation we all sat on the bed and talked about the great time we had. We had learned to catamaran. We had been on banana boat rides. We had parasailed and spent endless hours by the pool. When we asked the boys what had been the best part of the vacation for them, without a second's hesitation Nathan said, "When Jesus talked to me in the swimming pool!" From that time on, Nathan has been confident in the water: now he truly can swim like a fish! What the enemy meant for bad, God turned around for good. We no longer had to force Nathan into the shower (well, apart from the normal aversion to showers experienced by most prepubescent boys!). Every time I see Nathan in the pool, I thank God for what happened that day. When I wasn't watching, He was!

> I can assure you that while you do your best, God will fill in the gaps. Worry will profit neither you nor your children.

I wish all my experiences had such positive endings. I hesitate to tell you more stories in case they further cement my incompetence as a mother. But here goes! (At least you know that if God can look after *my* children, you can surely trust Him with yours.) Remember the trip to America? It was August 1998 and we were at Disney World on a Friday night during the US schools' summer break. There were about 100,000 people in the park that night. They were packed in so tightly that you had to hold hands as you walked in case you were separated. We had been through most of the park and Ashley yelled out to us to start heading for the entrance. It was nearly 10:30 at night, just minutes before the massive fireworks display. We pushed our way through the crowds, but we didn't get far as people were surging toward one of the squares to get a better look at the fireworks. We decided to go with the flow and paused to watch as the fireworks began.

The fireworks were spectacular, and Ashley asked me to grab the video camera from his backpack so he could film the fireworks in the night sky. I let go of Nathan's hand for a second to undo the backpack and hand Ashley the camera. But when I looked down again, Nathan was gone! He had kept walking, his eyes on the sky, and the crowd had engulfed him. Now, he would have only been a few feet away, but the noise from the fireworks and the voices around us made it impossible for him to hear our shouts. Our shouts turned to screams as we yelled his name. The people around us were oblivious to our rising panic. We frantically searched for him, pushing people aside, calling his name until we were hoarse. It was no use; the fireworks were ending and, as if controlled by an outside force, 100,000 people began to surge toward the entrance.

"Oh, God, Please, Please, Please, Keep Him Safe!"

Ashley and I decided to split up. I would go to the "Town Hall" and report Nathan missing and Ashley would race to the entrance to see if he could spot Nathan. I fought my way to the Town Hall, calling Nathan's name, trying to fight the panic that threatened to overwhelm me. "Now I know what other mothers go through when they lose a child," I thought desperately. "Will I ever see him again? Oh, God, please, please, please keep him safe!"

I reached the Town Hall and went straight to the counter. When the gentleman asked me if he could help, I burst into tears.

"Have you lost a child?" he asked. "Don't worry!" he assured me. "People lose over twenty children a week here and we always find them. Is this one yours?" He asked, pointing to a child scribbling on some paper, totally oblivious to the panic he was causing his parents.

I shook my head, so he asked me for a description. I started to describe Nathan: "About this tall, blonde hair, blue eyes…"

The radio crackled, the man answered, and then said, "They've just found a little girl. Excuse me, I'll just go and let her parents know."

I watched from across the room as the distraught faces of the parents turned to immediate joy; tears flowed as they heard the news that their daughter was safe. I secretly wished that was me.

The radio crackled again and this time the man flashed me a grin. "They've found him!" he said triumphantly. "He's over at the bus depot. They'll bring him here."

My legs felt weak.

"They've Found Him!"

Ashley had gone straight to the entrance but hadn't found him. He was hurrying up the steps of the Town Hall when I met him. I had rushed outside, searching the crowds for the first sign of Nathan. "They've found him!" I shouted as Ashley ran up the stairs toward me. It was another fifteen minutes before Nathan appeared, chatting away to a bus driver and inspecting the bus license he had been given.

When he saw Ashley he leapt into his arms and began to cry softly.

It wasn't until we were safely on the bus heading home that he began to tell us about his "adventure." When he had realized he was lost, he sat down on a park bench and began to cry. A few moments later he said to himself, "Nathan, this is not going to help you find your parents!" So he wiped his eyes, and just as he was about to get up again, a group of teenagers came up to him and asked him if he was lost. Because we had taught him never to talk to strangers, he said, "Nope!" and stood up and walked away. He had heard us saying that we were heading toward the entrance, so he thought he might be able to find us there.

> Many mothers become so consumed with the safety of their children that they produce children who are fearful and not confident in facing a world they are born to lead.

He reached the entrance and joined a family walking out the gates. Once he was out he walked the fifty meters to the bus depot and began reading the names of the resorts displayed on the top of the buses. After three buses had arrived and none of them bore the name "Disney Resort," he began to lose a little confidence. He walked over to one of the security staff standing at the bus station and said, "I'm lost." They immediately radioed his description to the Town Hall where I was anxiously waiting.

Fear Had Taken Root in His Little Life

Nathan was just eight years old at the time, and I wish I could say that he didn't suffer any bad effects from that experience, but he did. For years after that, whenever we were out shopping and I walked down a new aisle, I would hear his little voice quivering slightly with panic: "Mom! Mom!" It broke my heart as I realized fear had taken root in his little life. I also wish I could say that we prayed and God released him from that fear, but it didn't happen that way. It has faded slowly over the years, and yet I suspect it lingers still.

The fear remained for us as well. Even this week it surfaced again. We were in a crowded shopping mall in a foreign country, right in the middle of a festival where a concert was in full swing in the middle of the mall. Crowds of people milled around watching the spectacle. We sought shelter in a Burger King restaurant on the ground floor of the mall. As we finished eating, Ashley announced that he was strolling over to a watch shop within sight to have a look at a watch. None of us moved as we were too tired and hot, so Ashley went by himself. Nathan became impatient waiting for him and declared, "I'm going to tell Dad to hurry up."

Now, we assumed he had heard Ashley say he was walking over to a watch shop just a few feet away. Alas, this was not the case. Although Nathan had been sitting at the same table, he had actually been in another galaxy when Ashley said he was going to look at a watch. Instead, Nathan recalled a conversation some time earlier about sunglasses, so he headed off to find his father in a sunglasses shop. When Ashley returned without Nathan, we all glanced at each other and moaned in unison, "Oh, no!"

We immediately scattered and spent the next hour searching for Nathan. We called his room in the hotel, but there was no answer, so we kept looking. Finally we called the room again. This time his cheerful voice answered the phone. When he had not been able to locate Ashley, he wandered up a few floors looking for other sunglass shops. He has no sense of time passing, so after what must have been nearly an hour he walked back down to the Burger King restaurant. When he couldn't find us there, he decided to catch a bus back to the hotel without any idea of the commotion he had caused. He hadn't heard the phone ring the first time. "I must have been too engrossed in a television program," he said!

We Can't Be There for Our Kids All the Time

The truth is that no matter how hard we try, we can't be there for our kids all the time; we can't watch over them every second of the day. I recently relived the gut-wrenching fear that comes to (I'm sure) every mother when she tucks her newborn into his or her crib. I had forgotten what it was like to look at my peacefully sleeping baby and hope that the angel of death doesn't visit my home that night. I know what it is like to lie awake at night and fight the urge to just go check on my children one more time.

> No matter how hard we try, we can't watch over our kids every second of the day, but God can!

While I am certainly not advocating neglect, or even carelessness in your attention to safety, I am assuring you that while you do your best, God will fill in the gaps. Worry will profit neither you nor your children. You see, in hindsight, I believe God has even used Nathan's experiences for good. I have said before that he is a dreamer and that he tends to wander, lost in his thoughts and imagination. His fear has served to curb his wanderings a little. I still shudder to think what he'd be like if he hadn't gone through the experience of being lost!

I remember on one occasion I was sitting in the car outside a supermarket and I had just sent Nathan in to buy a loaf of bread. I only had a fifty-dollar bill on me, so I gave it to him to pay for the bread. Nathan appeared *thirty minutes later* with a whole bag full of groceries (and thankfully the bread!). When I questioned him, he told me he had decided he would grab a few other grocery items that he thought his family would love. The whole time he was in there he'd been planning in his head a special feast for us!

Do Your Best to Protect Your Children from Danger and Leave the Rest to God

Many mothers become so consumed with the safety of their children that they produce children who are fearful and who are not confident in facing a world they are born to lead. I see two results of this kind of overprotective behavior. First, some children get frustrated to the point that they go wild trying to break out of the "cotton wool world" their parents have made for them. They end up throwing themselves headlong into the danger their parents were trying to rescue them from. Second, some children embrace their over-safe world and never want to leave it, limiting them from being able to fulfill the potential for which they were born. You see, no matter how much you try, there are always going to be things that happen that are beyond your control. Control is a sign of a lack of trust. Do your best to protect your children from danger and harm, then leave the rest to God; He's far more vigilant than you'll ever be!

Chapter Nine

Discipline—the "D" Word

Trust Me, It Works!

Chapter Nine

Discipline—the "D" Word
Trust Me, It Works!

"Discipline your son, and he will give you peace;
he will bring delight to your soul."
—Proverbs 29:17 NIV

I think discipline would have to be one of the most misunderstood and frustrating aspects of parenting. Discipline is not meant to be a punishment for wrong *actions* but a correction of wrong *attitudes* that lead to wrong actions.

Sadly, too many of us have used discipline to:

- Vent our anger on our children
- Respond to the shame they have caused us because of their actions
- Punish them and make them pay for what they have done

- Manipulate them into feeling guilty for their misdemeanors.

When you understand how and why God disciplines, it is easier to understand the right way to discipline your child. The Bible says God disciplines those He loves. Proverbs 3:11–12 declares,

> *My child, don't ignore it when the* Lord *disciplines you, and don't be discouraged when he corrects you.* **For the** Lord **corrects those he loves, just as a father corrects a child in whom he delights.** (NLT)

> ### Discipline is not meant to be a punishment for wrong actions but a correction of wrong attitudes that lead to wrong actions.

The context of our Father's discipline is always His love for us. In fact, it says He *only* disciplines those He loves. That is powerful; it means the only motive behind His discipline is love. It is a love for us that is so deep He will risk "hurting" us in a controlled situation so that we are saved from hurting ourselves or others later in an uncontrolled situation.

Hebrews 12:7–9 tells us:

> *Endure hardship as discipline; God is treating you as sons.* **For what son is not disciplined by his father?** *If you are not disciplined (and everyone undergoes discipline), then you are illegitimate children and not true sons. Moreover, we have all had human fathers who disciplined us and we respected them for it. How much more should we submit to the Father of our spirits and live!* (NIV)

Discipline Makes You a True Son or Daughter of God

This verse says that discipline makes you a true son or daughter of God. If we refuse God's discipline, then by our choice we are placing ourselves outside the boundaries of His family, and we are declaring ourselves to be illegitimate sons and daughters. An illegitimate son or daughter never had the same rights to inheritance as legitimate children. In the context of this Scripture, illegitimate children were always on the outside, never quite fit in, and in some cases were sent away from home.

If we then refuse to apply discipline to our children, we offer them the same plight. Disciplining your children makes them feel a part of your family, assures them of your love for them, and instills in them the principles and values you have as a family. Without discipline, a child will feel outside of the family unit, will feel little or no security, and will quickly seek out the company of others who will make him or her feel "a part" of something, whether that be bad company at school, a gang, or another group in society with different morals and values than yours.

God disciplines us because He wants us to learn that His ways are best for us. He wants us to choose life instead of death, blessing instead of cursing. (See Deuteronomy 30:19.) He wants our feet to choose the right paths rather than the paths that lead to our destruction. He wants us to feel secure in His love.

If you struggle to discipline your children because your parents disciplined you in anger, and if, as a result, you don't trust your own levels of self-control, why don't you seek out some wise counsel and deal with the reservoir of emotions that threatens to take over when you are angry? Once the tank of emotions is drained, you will be able to look to God for help to wisely administer discipline according to His Word.

Another secret to successful discipline is not to wait until you are angry. Have you ever heard a conversation that went something like this?

> If we refuse God's discipline, then we are placing ourselves outside the boundaries of His family.

"Don't do that, Johnny!" warns Johnny's mom.

Johnny has learned not to listen until his parents warn him for the seventh time, so he ignores the initial request.

"Johnny, I SAID DON'T!"

"Johnny, no! Don't do that!"

"Johnny, you are being silly! Stop that, you'll hurt someone."

"Johnny, come here."

Johnny doesn't move.

"That's it, you are in big trouble if you do that once more!"

"Johnny, I said come here. You are going to be in big trouble when your dad gets home."

"Get over here now and do as you are told!"

"I'm warning you!"

"STOP IT NOW!"

Johnny hears the anger beginning to build in his mom's voice and runs off. The warnings she started half an hour ago have been ineffective, and the friend that she was chatting to has moved away, made uncomfortable by the impending confrontation. Johnny's mom runs after him, yanks his arm, and belts him wherever she can make contact with him. He had started screaming long before his mom reached him. His scream now becomes a shriek, and she knows that once again she has lost the battle. People are watching and she wishes that just for once Johnny would do as he was told. She reluctantly lets go of his arm, feeling like a failure and wondering guiltily where she went wrong.

What should have happened is this: Mom sees that Johnny's behavior is unacceptable according to the values she wants to instill into her child. She warns him not to repeat the behavior. If the behavior is repeated, she calmly and without anger administers discipline. Then she takes a moment to cuddle Johnny and tells him why what he did is not acceptable. She elicits an apology from him…to her and to God.

Discipline Should Be a Deterrent to Further Disobedience

If Johnny had been disciplined the very first time he did what his mom had asked him not to do, his mom would have saved herself the embarrassment and the emotional drain of having to nag him until she became so angry she couldn't help but react. She should be reinforcing to Johnny that the next time she asks him not to do something, he had better do as he is told, as there will be immediate consequences. Those consequences should be strong enough to deter him from making the wrong choice again. Incorrect or ineffective discipline just aggravates a child (as it would an adult!) and, instead of being a deterrent, acts as fuel on the fire of disobedience. Discipline should be a deterrent to further disobedience. It should not produce anger or frustration within the child.

Children are smarter than we ever give them credit for. Don't try to discipline or change the way you discipline until you have settled the issue thoroughly in your heart and have discussed it with your spouse. If you are unsure about what you are doing, if you feel sorry for the child, if you feel that the behavior is cute and really shouldn't be punished, or if you are not sure that what you are doing is the right thing, then your child will spot you coming a mile away. Your children will sense your reticence and pounce mercilessly on your indecision. They will make you feel guilty. They will try to manipulate you. They will try their hardest to prove to you that what you are doing won't work. So set your face like flint and determine to follow the patterns God has set in His Word. Do this together with your partner; discuss it before you need to use it, and go in confidently even when you are not sure what to do.

> Children will make you feel guilty. They will try to manipulate you. So determine to follow the patterns God has set in His Word.

Teenagers can test you in this area like no one else. If you ask them who was responsible for a misbehavior, each of them will say the other one was. Many times I have spent hours trying to get to the bottom of something, but now I just send them both to their rooms and tell them that, since I can't work out who was to blame, they will both be disciplined until the matter can be solved. I give them the liberty to talk it out with one another. It generally takes less than ten minutes before the matter is resolved, often both of them owning up to their part, resolving the issue between them, and emerging best of friends again...until the next time!

None of us likes to discipline our children. It is not something we take pleasure in. Rather, it is something we do knowing it will reap a harvest of obedience later on. Proverbs 29:15 says, *"The rod and rebuke* [correction and punishment] *give wisdom, but a child left to himself brings shame to his mother."*

That's so true. If you are procrastinating about discipline, just think about the shame your children will bring you if they are left to themselves. I know some women I would love to build a friendship with, but I hesitate to do so because their children are undisciplined and wild. Time spent with them is interrupted every two minutes by "Don't do that!" and "Stop that, Johnny!" and "Come here now!" and "I'm warning you!" I'm completely worn out after half an hour. I can only imagine how they feel!

Some fear disciplining their children will make their children hate them. Proverbs 29:17 promises: *"Discipline your children, and they will give you happiness and peace of mind"* (NLT). When we discipline our children according to the pattern God set out for us—the pattern He uses on us—the result will be respect, not hatred! In fact, the Bible says that if God doesn't discipline you, He doesn't love you or delight in you! Because He loves all of us, we all feel His discipline and correction.

I see some parents who refrain from discipline, stating that they love their children too much to do anything that would cause them pain. In actual fact, many of these parents are too fearful to discipline because they either fear losing their self-control while disciplining (having been disciplined in anger by their own parents and not wanting to repeat the same mistake), or they are afraid that their children will not love them if they discipline them. Either way, the child will be the one who misses out.

Discipline: to Train or Educate

The word *discipline* here in Proverbs 29:17 is the word *pahee-di'-ah,* which literally means "to train or educate through disciplinary correction." In other words, the whole purpose of God's discipline is to train and educate us in the right ways to live. Discipline should be a training or educational process rather than a punishment. According to this verse, there are two wrong responses to discipline: to ignore it and to become discouraged by it. At times I've seen both these reactions in my own boys. On occasions they have chosen to shut down and totally ignore me, or they have gone to the other extreme and put on the "victim show": "I'm hopeless!" or "You don't really love me!"

> Discipline reaps a harvest of obedience later on. Correction and punishment make children wise, but those left alone will disgrace their mother.

Both these responses are wrong. We need to understand that the context of God's discipline is always love. He only disciplines those He loves. So the context of our discipline should always be the same. When love for our children is the focus of our discipline, we can see beyond the here and now, beyond the anger they have stirred in us, and we can look to their future. You see, discipline is all about training for the future. We can also see beyond their wrong responses to our discipline and maintain our focus until these attitudes are corrected.

Every Action Has a Consequence

The real purpose of discipline is to teach a child that every action has a consequence. For example, wrong actions have painful consequences. Wrong actions break God's laws. God Himself has said that when we do wrong we must face the consequences. When we choose to do wrong, we also choose the consequences attached to that wrong action.

God is not like a mean parent who is waiting for us to do wrong and then, depending on what mood he is in that day, metes out punishment on us. No! In essence, we choose our punishment when we choose our behavior. The consequences are attached to the wrong behavior we have chosen. God allows us to feel those consequences so that we will be reluctant to repeat the wrong behavior. The consequences are there to deter us from repeating the same behavior and to correct us and train us to choose the right way over the wrong way. It's the same with our children. We need to make sure the consequences of wrong actions are sufficiently uncomfortable to make them hesitate before repeating the offense.

> The context of God's discipline is always love. He only disciplines those He loves.

Sometimes Discipline Is Inconvenient

One of my sons once took a packet of candy through a supermarket checkout without telling me. As a consequence, neither he nor I paid for it. I only noticed the candy when we arrived home. About six years old, he was old enough to know better, so I took him back to the supermarket, found the woman who had served us, and explained what had happened.

I asked him to give the candy back to her, to apologize to her for taking it without paying, and then to also pay her out of his own pocket money the amount the candy would have cost. Let me tell you, this was hard for me to do too! I did not have time that day. And I was embarrassed as I was trying to explain to a cashier why it was important that my son return to pay for the half-eaten candy and she kept saying, "It's fine. Don't worry." Trust me, it would have been a lot easier for me to deal with it myself. But I promise you, the consequences of stopping a repeat offense were far more successful than if I had administered justice myself.

Sometimes discipline is inconvenient at the time, but it will save you heartbreak later on! As a parent, I believe God has given me opportunities to step in and administer discipline that arrests wrong behavior before it takes too much control of my children...even when on occasions I have had no idea about what was happening.

I remember one day being frustrated looking for our cordless telephone. It wasn't in its cradle, so I had searched the entire house wanting to make a phone call. In desperation I pressed the intercom button to send a signal to the phone so that a beeping sound would help me locate it. As I pressed the button, I was suddenly linked to a phone conversation taking place. I heard teenage girls giggling and then I heard my son's voice and the voice of a friend. I heard a string of profanities come from the other boy's mouth, and then my son followed that with words that should never have come from his mouth. I froze, and then I discovered the location of the missing phone when one of the female voices asked, "Where are you?"

"Leaning over my neighbor's fence," my son answered.

"Come and meet us in the park," they urged.

I didn't wait to hear any more. I marched outside and interrupted their little telephone rendezvous as only a mother can. Needless to say, we talked that one through then and there. I put a stop to my son meeting with the older boy until they had both matured enough to be good company for one another. My son actually thanked me for intervening and, although he had been punished, he felt almost relieved that I had stepped in because he was beginning to feel a little out of his depth.

I have considered trying to eavesdrop over the phone since, but I couldn't interrupt a conversation, even if I wanted to because I don't know how I did it! I believe God allows us to get caught sometimes to pull us up. He gives us a reality check to stop us in our tracks before our behavior becomes destructive to ourselves or to others. Of course, we all have a choice to listen or not to God's correction. Sadly, far too many people make the wrong choices. It just means the next lesson that presents itself will be harder to learn if wrong behavior has become habitual and if our conscience has been dulled.

> It is important to make sure our children understand what repentance means. They need to get their hearts right with God.

That's why it is so important to me to make sure my children understand what repentance means; that they understand they have not only hurt or disobeyed me, they have also disobeyed God. Not only do they need to say sorry to me, but more importantly, they need to get their hearts right with God. True repentance will bring change. Just being sorry for getting caught or being sorry because they don't like the consequences will not be enough to change them.

I'm not pretending that discipline is easy. It's not! It's hard work! Just being consistent day after day can wear you out and tempt you to give up. But let me assure you, you will reap the rewards of your labor if you don't give up and if you continue to apply discipline in the way that God has outlined for us in His Word.

Chapter Ten

Final Thoughts
In an Ideal World...

Final Thoughts
In an Ideal World...

> *"The future belongs to those who believe*
> *in the beauty of their dreams."*
> *— Eleanor Roosevelt*

*I*n an ideal world, the best environment for parenting exists when a husband and wife love each other deeply, agree on the principles of parenting, and present a united front to their children. A unified front is hard to penetrate. In an ideal world, a mother rises at the first sound of her children, greets the day with enthusiasm, and never once wishes to be anywhere else but with her husband and brood of young. In an ideal world, every child strives to do what is right and— okay, I'll stop the rubbish!

Women Parenting Alone Are among the Strongest and Noblest on This Planet

None of us lives in an ideal world! The reality is that not all of you will have the benefit of a wonderful, supportive husband (as I have had). Some of you may even be parenting alone, without the support of your children's father. If you are, you belong to a company of women who are among the strongest and noblest on this planet; a company of women whose self-sacrifice and determination make the rest of us seem soft. I admire your tenacity and, although you may not have chosen to do life this way, I know that if you ask God for strength, enough for one day at a time, He will give it to you. If you read through the Bible, God's heart is constantly shown toward the fatherless. He promises to protect them and fight for them.

> **Throughout the Bible, God's heart is shown toward the fatherless. He promises to protect them and fight for them.**

On the cross Jesus knew what it was like to be forsaken by His Father. He called out as He was dying, *"My God, my God, why have you forsaken me?"* (Matthew 27:46 NIV). Psalm 68:5-6 says this:

> [He is a] *Father to the fatherless, defender of widows—this is God, whose dwelling is holy. God places the lonely in families; He sets the prisoners free and gives them joy.* (NLT)

Don't lose heart! You may *feel* alone, but you do not have to *be* alone! Find a great church and become planted in God's house. Allow His family to be your family and God to be your husband.

Do Not Compare Yourself with Others

The truth is that all our situations are as unique as we are. One of the worst things we do as parents is constantly compare ourselves and our children with others.

I have an older sister who is a devoted and wonderful mother. Her children were, and still are, impeccably well-behaved. They have now grown into adulthood and are still the nicest "kids" you'll ever meet. They are all involved in the youth group at our church and contribute greatly to the world around them. It was not easy following my sister's example! My boys were wild from the day they were born. They seemed to sense every opportunity for mischief and seize it with both hands. At family gatherings it was *my* children who painted mud on my sister's walls, it was *my* children who climbed the lemon tree and threw lemons over the neighbor's fence, and it was *my* son who, on one occasion, carved a lump out of my sister's outdoor furniture set with his knife! (Does that make you feel a bit better?) I would often despair and be tempted to force my children into a mold that they could never fit, a mold that would make me feel better as a mother.

There is no worse motivation for parenting than trying to make your children into people who will make you feel better about yourself.

The truth is that your children have your genes! Neither Ashley nor I are placid or laid back. Why on earth did we expect our children to be something we are not?!

Your Children Were Given to You, Not to the Girl Next Door

Your children are a gift from God; they were given to you, not to the girl next door, nor to the woman who frowns at you in the supermarket! You are the best mother for them: believe it and be her! Remember, God searched the entire planet looking for the best mother for your children. He looked for someone who would take them for Him and nurture and train them so that they would become all that He wanted them to be...and He chose you!

So don't look at the mother across the road and wish you were she, or look at someone else's children and feel guilty because your own seem so wild in comparison. I have known children who behaved immaculately and then later in their teenage years rebelled because it wasn't character they were functioning from; it was fear.

You rarely get to see the mistakes other people make; most often you just see the results of those mistakes. People's true parenting styles usually don't emerge until they are behind closed doors, when no one else is watching. What you see now is what they want you to see—not a sound basis for comparison at all! So rise up, woman of God! Square your shoulders, take a deep breath, take hold of God's hand, and be the very best mom that you can be!

Jane Evans

J ane Evans and her husband, Ashley, are the senior pastors of Paradise Community Church in Adelaide, South Australia. This vibrant church is one of the largest and most successful in Australia, ministering to more than six thousand people each weekend. Jane leads and oversees more than one hundred paid full-time staff and more than one thousand volunteers in her role as a senior pastor.

Jane is a dynamic speaker, leader, and motivator. She is highly respected and is a much sought-after conference speaker who has an intense and passionate ability to powerfully communicate truth and life into her audiences. She speaks regularly on TV in the Australian and American markets and is considered one of the emerging voices to women all over the world.

Jane possesses tremendous versatility and is able to speak with authority on a broad range of topics. The mother of two teenagers and a toddler, she is a full-time minister who travels the world speaking and teaching. Her background as a counselor to thousands of women and her success at helping countless women overcome the effects of abuse and other life-altering problems help her understand first-hand the issues facing ordinary people. One of Jane's amazing gifts is perception and an ability to speak with piercing accuracy into the lives of people. She is personable, warm, and able to relate to people of all ages. She has great honesty and sensitivity, and she tackles the easy and difficult areas of life with the same boldness and openness. One of Jane's great characteristics is her humor, which she uses powerfully to engage her audiences and penetrate their hearts.

She is also on the board of directors for Compassion Australia and is the South Australian Director of Australian Christian Women.

Along with Ashley, Jane's ministry includes the challenging and fruitful area of managing their household and raising their three sons, Mark, Nathan, and Benjamin, aged eighteen, sixteen, and four.

www.janeevans.org

For speaking engagements and feedback, please e-mail
jane.evans@paradise.asn.au

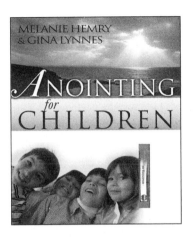

Anointing for Children
Melanie Hemry and Gina Lynnes

The devil is out to get our children. Most of us have already figured
that out. What we need to know is how to keep them out of
his hands. Find out how other determined parents have done it.
Discover the scriptural truths that inspired them and witness the
miracles that happened in their children's lives as they stepped out
in faith on God's Word. Whether you're struggling with barrenness,
hoping to have a baby, needing healing for your child, or praying for
a prodigal to come home, *Anointing for Children* has a message of
hope and faith for you.

ISBN: 978-0-88368-686-7 • Gift Book • 192 pages
comes with a 1 mL vial of pomegranate-scented anointing oil

WHITAKER
HOUSE

www.whitakerhouse.com

Raising Children on Purpose
Wesley H. Fleming

Who's raising your children?
As parents, we want our children to be motivated, goal-oriented, responsible, and passionate about their life and faith...we want them to know the way they are to go. Disciplining your children can be an expression of love for them.
Wes Fleming's *Raising Children on Purpose* offers practical advice in an easy-to-understand manner with a sprinkling of humor. By following these loving guidelines, you can raise your children to become PEAK PERFORMERS!

ISBN: 978-0-88368-997-4 • Trade • 224 pages

www.whitakerhouse.com

Raising Your Children for Christ
Andrew Murray

Children are gifts from the Lord. In this practical guide to parenting, Andrew Murray shows the essential qualities of being a parent who loves the Lord. He also shows you how to build your family in the Lord, alleviate stressful family situations, direct your children's steps, and see the needs of your family met. In this book, you will find biblical advice and God's promises on how you can shape and mold the lives of your children for eternity!

ISBN: 978-0-88368-045-2 • Mass Market
320 pages

Spiritual Parenting
Charles H. Spurgeon

Your child is worth all your time, money, heartaches, and effort because your child can make a difference in this world. From the depths of his God-given wisdom, Charles Spurgeon shows how you can establish a secure, nurturing, Christ-centered home in which to grow strong, healthy, and happy families. Here is encouragement and advice to parents on guiding the spiritual development of children from infancy through young adulthood.

ISBN: 978-0-88368-959-2 • Trade • 176 pages

www.whitakerhouse.com

Little Hickman Creek Series

Loving Liza Jane

Liza Jane Merriwether had come to Little Hickman Creek, Kentucky, to teach. She had a lot of love to give to her students. She just hadn't reckoned on the handsome stranger with two adorable little girls and a heart of gold that was big enough for one more.

Ben Broughton missed his wife, but he was doing the best he could to raise his two daughters alone. Still, he had to admit that he needed help, which is why he wrote to the Marriage Made in Heaven Agency for a mail-order bride. While he was waiting for a response, would he overlook the perfect wife that God had practically dropped in his lap?

ISBN: 978-0-88368-816-8 • Trade • 368 pages

Sarah, My Beloved

Sarah Woodward has come to Kentucky as a mail-order bride. But when she steps off the stage coach, the man who contacted her through the Marriage Made in Heaven Agency informs her that he has fallen in love with and wed another woman. With her usual stubborn determination, she refuses to leave until she finds out what God's reason is. Rocky Callahan's sister has died, leaving him with two young children to take care of. When he meets the fiery Sarah, he proposes the answer to both their problems—a marriage in name only. Can he let go of the pain in his past and trust God's plan for his life? Will she leave him or will they actually find a marriage made in heaven?

ISBN: 978-0-88368-425-2 • Trade • 368 pages

Courting Emma

Twenty-eight-year-old Emma Browning has experienced a good deal of life in her young age. Proprietor of Emma's Boardinghouse, she is "mother" to an array of brawny, unkempt, often rowdy characters. Though many men would like to get to know the steely, hard-edged, yet surprisingly lovely proprietor, none has truly succeeded. That is, not until the town's new pastor, Jonathan Atkins, takes up residence in the boardinghouse.

ISBN: 978-1-60374-020-3 • **Available Spring 2008**

WHITAKER HOUSE

www.whitakerhouse.com